My Journey To Freedom

Born Amish… A True Story

Mattie Mullet

Copyright © 2011 Mattie Mullet

All rights reserved. Without limiting the rights under copyright reserved above, no part of this publication may be reproduced, stored in or introduced into a retrieval system, or transmitted, in any form or by any means (electronic, mechanical, photocopying, recording or otherwise), without the prior written permission of both the copyright owner and the above publisher of this book.

This publication is designed to provide accurate and authoritative information in regard to the subject matter covered. It is sold with the understanding that the publisher is not engaged in rendering legal, accounting, or other professional service. If legal advice or other expert assistance is required, the services of a competent professional person should be sought. —*From a Declaration of Principles Jointly Adopted by a Committee of the American Bar Association and a Committee of Publishers and Associations.*

Printed in the United States of America

ISBN 978-1-105-196348

TABLE OF CONTENTS

		Page
Acknowledgments		5
Foreword		7
Chapter 1	Some Background History of the Amish	9
Chapter 2	My Family Background	19
Chapter 3	Childhood Memories	27
Chapter 4	Schooling and Education	35
Chapter 5	Out-of-School	43
Chapter 6	Teen Years	47
Chapter 7	Courtship and Wedding	67
Chapter 8	Marriage Woes in the Early Years	73
Chapter 9	More of the Early Years	81
Chapter 10	New Baby Woes	85

Chapter 11	More Indiana Stories	**95**
Chapter 12	Move to Clinton, Michigan	**105**
Chapter 13	Battered Wife	**125**
Chapter 14	Neighbor's Kindness	**135**
Chapter 15	Clinton and Youth	**139**
Chapter 16	Change: Another Story	**147**
Chapter 17	Fearful Times at Church	**151**
Chapter18	Move to Austin, Michigan	**161**
Chapter 19	My Mother's Death	**173**
Chapter 20	Move to Maxville	**185**
Chapter 21	Charlotte Wedding	**199**
Chapter 22	Rumors and Conversions	**217**
About The Author		**227**

ACKNOWLEDGMENTS

First, I want to thank my Lord and Savior, Jesus Christ, for being my constant companion during my journey to freedom. I love all my children, but special thanks to Lorene and Aden and their family, who provided a safe place for me while I was on my healing journey. To Betty, whom I lived with while writing this book, thank you for supporting and encouraging me, and just being there during the tough times. Special thanks to all the Corrie family who "adopted" me when I had no-one and especially to Stan and Teresa, for encouraging me to write and believing in me. Last, but not least, I want to thank my pastors, Jerry and Patsy Spratt and the special people in the congregation who also helped in my healing. It truly has been a safe sanctuary filled with God's presence.

FOREWORD

I hope this book helps to clear up misconceptions and confusion about the Amish. I have read and heard things that aren't true or even come close to the whole truth. This book is not written to harm anyone, but to provide information so that others might better understand how to help Amish people. There will be things written that don't apply to every community, but it's very real and true in the communities I lived in.

My family had been Amish for generations. At age 51, I did the unthinkable. I left everything I had ever known. That would've been impossible to do with all the shunning that followed. If it hadn't been for my precious Jesus, I never would have found the strength to leave.

Now, it is my heart's sincere desire that everybody come to the saving knowledge of Jesus Christ and experience the joy of salvation, and that includes my loved ones, the Amish.

The names and places have been changed in this book to protect the privacy of the people concerned. The actual events, however, are real.

CHAPTER ONE

Once upon a time… is how Fairy Tales and many stories begin. This book is not a Fairy Tale nor is it fiction. It is the truth as I lived it.

Some Background History of the Amish

I come from generations of Amish. I think that would be true of almost any Amish person, because it's extremely rare that an outsider comes in and becomes a member. Most attempts that have been made to join were due to ignorance of what it's like on the inside. The Amish population is growing rapidly because of their large families and the small percentage that leave.

According to Wikipedia: The **Amish** (/'a: mɪʃ/ *Amish*; Pennsylvania Dutch: *Amisch*, German: *Amische*), sometimes referred to as **Amish,** are a group of Christian church fellowships that form a subgroup of the Mennonite churches. The Amish are known for simple living, plain dress, and reluctance to adopt many conveniences of modern technology.

There are many stories and books in the world about the history of the Amish so I will just write the basics. Jacob Ammon was a young man involved in the Mennonite church. In 1693, he broke away and started the Amish church. One of the issues he had was about banning and shunning. He didn't think the Mennonites were doing it according to Scripture. Ironically, he started banning and shunning anyone in the church who didn't believe like he did. Then, he also added many rules that, supposedly, would keep them, his followers, separate from the world.

One example was using hooks and eyes, instead of buttons, on the men's coats and jackets. Ammon considered the men in the military to be of the world and, in those days, they had extra-large buttons on their uniforms. The men are allowed to have small buttons on their shirts and pants. They wear beards but no mustaches, because in Ammon's days worldly men wore them in stylish fashions.

Women are not allowed to have any buttons, snaps, or any means to close their dresses and fasten their capes and aprons, except with straight pins. The pins are a little over an inch long. The rules vary in communities about whether the pins have to be placed up and down or if they may be crossways down the front of the cape. Little girls wear dresses that fasten in the back and they can have buttons, until about 10 years old when they wear dresses like the adults.

It would take up too much space and time to explain all the many, many rules. The rules are passed down and kept rather rigidly. They do vary in communities, but if you live in a more conservative community, you are taught it's wrong to move to a more liberal one. Each community has its own rules that were established by a small group of people who started the community.

Where I grew up, the community burgeoned into 6 districts, with an average of 20 to 25 families in each one, allowing them to meet in houses for church services. Clinton, Michigan had 11 districts when last I heard, but not often does a community get that large, due to families moving out. Many move to other communities because of abuse from the church, such as a bishop acting like a tyrant causing much turmoil, or disunity, splits and ill feelings, or some just want more liberty and others start new groups.

Church service is held in homes every two weeks, so that the ministers and the people can attend other districts. Each district has 1 bishop, 2 ministers and 1 deacon.

The bishops, ministers and deacons all get together at least twice a year to discuss rules and try to agree on various issues and how to keep things under control. Many times they have serious disagreements and walk away with ill feelings toward each other.

Amish mostly use the King James Version of the Bible but read and preach it in the German language. Some can pronounce the words well enough, but their understanding of the meaning is limited. They really hang tight to the traditions of their forefathers believing somehow that the German language is more holy.

Unlike in China, girl babies are not viewed differently from boy babies. They seem to have the same value in the Amish culture. There is a tendency for husbands to control and dominate their wives, mostly due to taking the Bible out of context. Some also learn it from their dad's example. However, incest and sexual abuse have been increasing, as the population grows.

I'm so thankful that I grew up in a family where that didn't happen to me. Someone who left the Amish told us, after the family was out of the community, their children confessed to sexual activity. The children had been involved with the neighbor children at a pre-adolescent age.

The parents weren't aware that anything was going on. Sometimes, the neighbors would get together and while the parents were visiting, the children would be doing forbidden things with each other. It could be out in the barn or another building, and some of the children were pretty small. Also, a minister's young sons had told some ex-Amish how the boys molested their little sisters while the girls sat on their laps in the back seat of the double buggy, on the way to church.

If the incidents included members of the church, they would be punished with the worst of the punishments and that would be "the ban" for several weeks. Banning means you are no longer a member and you cannot associate or eat with anyone who is a member. Generally, the ban lasts for two weeks, sometimes four weeks, depending on the person's attitude or misdeed. If the person is rebellious or not willing to repent, he will not be taken in as a member again until he repents. Many times a person has already repented, but he will still be banned for two weeks. Shunning is only practiced while a person is banned. A person is shunned if he leaves the Amish, but he can become a member again if he comes back and repents. However, if he has been baptized again he is shunned permanently.

A funeral is different from occasions like weddings where people are invited. "English" (someone who is not Amish), ex-Amish, or anyone else may attend a funeral. That person, or persons, is not seated with the relatives but is seated in the back or in another room somewhere.

Very few Amish have ever been punished by the law of the land, since they are non-resistant. This means the Amish don't believe in going to war, or fighting in court or using the law of the land. They believe their way of punishment is sufficient. I really feel for the victims. I wish there was some sort of help or counseling for them.

The Amish usually don't press charges or turn anyone in, not even for sexual abuse. I think if I did such a thing, I would probably be considered a hateful, vengeful person, as bad as the one I turned in. Taking issues outside the church is a big offense.

Bestiality was quite common and was punished with the ban for two weeks. One bishop put himself under the ban twice. In his case, he had repented, but did it again about a year later.

A person's conscience would bother them so badly they would confess the sin in church. The ban was used for a few weeks because it made offenders feel they were forgiven. This is a common practice among most communities.

CHAPTER TWO

My Family Background

My maiden name was Mattie J. Raber. I was born in 1952.

Father:	Joseph J. Raber	1908
First Wife:	Amanda Miller	
Half-Siblings:	Jonas	1931
	Vernon	1932
	Ben	1935
	John	1936
	Ella	1937
	Anna	1938
Mother:	Marie Coblentz	1918
Siblings:	Atlee	1953
	Marvin	1954
	Malinda	1955
	Joseph	1956
	Dora	1960

Jonas's wife Sara died in 1995, of a brain aneurysm, shortly after he was ordained bishop. He remarried a widow named Martha. Her deceased husband had also been a bishop.

My parents lived in Hilton County, Virginia, where I was born.

In March of 1953, we moved to a 200 acre farm they purchased in Butler County, Indiana. I was one year old at the time. My brother, Atlee, was born a month later. I can't imagine how Mother and the rest of the family must have felt moving so far, having never seen the farm. Hilton County was very hilly with nice scenery; Butler County was flat and dull, but the farmland was very productive.

It was a short time later that my half-brother, John, ran away and went back to Virginia. He was only 17 years old and it broke my dad's heart. He had lived with my father and my mother, who was his stepmother, because the custom is for the children to stay under the same roof with the father until they are 21 years old or get married. I didn't know much about John's life after he left, but when he came back to visit, he had a car and "English" clothes. The Amish called everyone who was outside our culture an "Englisher." His attire was considered liberal or "up high in dress". He wore custom tailored tight pants and fancy shirts.

John married an Amish girl, but my dad resented the idea of him becoming a member of the church where she belonged. This was one of the many different levels of churches that had split off from the original communities in Hilton County. They all have different rules, and when someone goes to a more liberal church, they are considered "proud" and "rebellious."

We children would be just awestruck when they came to visit. John's wife, Mary, was labeled *stolz* or fancy, almost proud, all based on outward appearance. She wore shorter dresses, smaller, fancier caps that didn't cover as much of her hair, plastic frame glasses, and their children were given two names, such as Susie Kay, which was considered worldly! Her dress was considered liberal or "up high in dress." Dad was not too happy. John and dad would have their discussions about John and Mary moving to a "lower" church, but they ended up moving to New York to a New Order Amish church, which was more progressive.

The dress part looked better, but they had electricity and phones, plus every modern convenience, except cars. John became a minister there.

We visited them when I was about 21 years old. It was the first time in my life that I heard anyone pray without a prayer book. John just made it up like he was talking to you and me. We thought he'd gone off the deep end!

After my brother, Atlee, was born a year after me, my mother was in bed for about six months. She had complications from the birth called milk leg, which left her paralyzed in one leg. Her leg functioned normally after six months. I think the medical term for milk leg is "phlebitis."So, it was a good thing to have my half-sisters, Ella and Anna, there to do the work.

My father's first wife, Amanda, died when Anna, the youngest, was 12 years old. I barely remember when Ella got married. I have more memories of Anna, since I was eight years old when she got married. She was strong and a hard worker which was what my mother needed because she was always frail from an illness she had before she married. Also, she was having babies every year now by Caesarian section, which didn't help matters any.

When I think of Anna back then, I still see her standing at the ironing board, doing the weekly ironing, which took hours. We used a heavy gas iron, which usually gave us a bad headache from gas fumes. The white capes, aprons and caps that we wore to church had to be starched. One cap could take from thirty minutes to one hour to get it right.

My little brothers loved to tease Anna while she was ironing and she would get upset and tell them to quit. Of course, they loved her responses and things heated up until Anna, suddenly, chased after them around the house. She'd grab them by the seat of their pants, one in each hand, and she'd carry them that way while they were laughing and kicking.

My half-brother, Jonas, was married soon after I was born. Later, they moved to Indiana, too, and had 15 children. He became a minister and later, a bishop.

My siblings, their children and I often played together. I have some memories of my half-brother, Ben, before he got married. He had to tolerate us when we would jump up and down on his back, while he was trying to rest on the living room floor. That was after supper when the work was done. After he married, they moved to a house across the road and helped with the farming, for a percentage. We helped with milking the cows as soon as we were old enough, about six years old. Ben was very busy on the farm, and seemed to be half running all the time. Ben's wife, Ida, taught us many songs and funny little poems, mostly while we were milking.

One tragedy happened when I was 9 years old: my half-sister Ella's oldest child, Anna, who was three years old at the time, died from burns. Her clothes caught on fire from a gas lamp. That was a traumatic experience for all of us; I was very fond of her.

In 1980, there was another family tragedy when my half-sister Anna's oldest son, Raymond, was killed at six years old. He was walking to school on a windy, winter day, when his hat blew off. As he made a dash for it, he ran in front of an oncoming milk truck. He was killed instantly. These parents waited 14 years before God gave them children, so it was especially hard for them. They were blessed with three other boys.

Family Members

I had 7 children, my brother Atlee had 9 and my brother Marvin had 14, our sister Malinda had 8 and our brother Joseph had 8. Our sister Dora had 12.

These are my children:
Betty (single), Alfred (8 children), Lorene (7 children), Ivan (6 children), Miriam (5 children), Marilyn (4 children), David (no children)

I have 31 wonderful grandchildren. The two oldest grandchildren were born only a week apart. They are 15 years old now.

CHAPTER THREE

Childhood Memories

I have some memories that will help you know my family better. It was rare that my dad could spend a Sunday at home, because there were times when he had to take care of another district that didn't have a bishop yet.

So, on the in-between Sunday, my mother would have us read out of the German Bible, taking turns, two verses at a time. After we sang a few German songs, we could go out and play.

On one particular Sunday, when I was about 11 years old, my dad was home, and after our usual devotions, he told us to play very quietly, because he wanted to sleep. He often had trouble sleeping, because of church problems, etc., and he'd get irritated or upset if he was awakened from a much needed nap.

Well, we were in the back yard and I completely forgot myself and was loudly shouting to my brothers. I was under the small apple tree and was, suddenly, surprised when my dad appeared, grabbed me and gave me a spanking, and without saying one word, he went back inside. At first, I couldn't understand why. Finally, it sank in, what I'd done.

It was rare that he gave spankings in that fashion. Usually, he'd take us into the bedroom and explain the offence and we knew we had it coming. Well, my siblings and I weren't very happy to have to be so quiet, so we went up in the haymow; we were all in one accord and had an all-out pity party!

We all had a story to tell about some injustice, real or imagined, that our terrible dad had done to us! Suddenly, we saw dad peeping around the opening to the straw shed, on his hands and knees. I'm certain he heard it all, but he was laughing and he joined us and we had a fun time. Needless to say, all our grievances and woes dissipated into thin air!

My mother was not strong physically, so she was very poor at disciplining us and she knew it, and always said she didn't have the strength to do it, even though she really wanted to. She felt very badly about it and I know she made up for it in prayers for us. She was very kind and loving and many little kindnesses were done to us. She had a special plate she'd use to bring us food when we were sick in bed, and brought us all the comforts she could. She could find joy in the smallest things!

My mother carried a little narrow strap in her dress pocket. Often she didn't have enough strength to make that very effective either, especially for the boys. I'm so thankful that my dad took care of her and spent a lot of money for her health, as well as mine. I wish I could've known them without the heavy burden of him being bishop and tied down with religious bondage.

Cousins and Kinship

My maternal grandfather, Levi Coblentz, died when I was six years old. I remember we went on a train to Hilton County, Virginia, to the funeral. When we arrived, we went into the bedroom where his remains lay, for a final viewing. My grandparents lived in a separate little house with my aunt, so my cousins were closer to grandfather. I saw my aunts and uncles were crying.

When I noticed my cousin, Nelson, who was my age, crying, I tried my best to get some tears to come out, but I couldn't make myself cry.

When my dad saw how my face was screwed up, he asked me, "What's wrong?"

"Nothing," I said. I wondered why he didn't ask the others what was wrong.

My half-brother, Vernon, lived in a state hospital in Akron. I only saw him once in my life, when we went to my maternal grandma Mattie Coblentz's funeral, when I was 14 years old.

We had traveled by train and stayed about two weeks, and that was enough to wish our parents had never moved! We cousins looked past our differences in dress (they were more liberal than we were), and we discovered such kindred spirits amongst us and had terrific fun. Unfortunately, we only saw each other a few times while growing up.

Some of our aunts and uncles visited on rare occasions. When aunt Lydia and uncle Andy Yoder visited, when I was 15 years old, they brought their family of four boys and one girl. I won't forget the fun we had and how lonely it was when they went home. It seemed so dull and dead when I went back to work that Monday morning, carrying water to heat for the wringer washer.

At that time, we had two hand pumps, one on each end of the kitchen sink. One was for drinking water and the other was out of a cistern where the rainwater was caught. We would place milk pails under that pump and fill them, then carry them two at a time, through the kitchen, and out the back door to the washhouse. There we emptied them into a large cast iron kettle and a fire was built underneath to heat the water. It took quite a few trips to get that kettle filled. We liked using the rainwater to wash our hair because it got so soft and shiny. The soft rainwater got the clothes cleaner, too.

When I was somewhere between age 13 and 15 years old, my half-brother, Ben, helped us rig up something that gave us hours of enjoyment. He fastened a long, heavy rope to a big limb, way up high in a large tree behind the washhouse. A gunny sack was filled with straw and tied to the other end of the rope. We put a ladder against the washhouse and dragged the gunny sack with us to the roof. Then, we straddled it, hung onto the rope, lifted our feet, and we were off to the ride of our lives! It seemed like we were flying right into the clouds! I watched the others for quite some time before I got brave enough to try it.

CHAPTER FOUR

Schooling and Education

We started going to school at age six in a one room schoolhouse. At that time, we still had state certified non-Amish, teachers. All eight grades were taught in that one room and it held about 25 children.

We had to walk one and a half miles, but the neighbor children who lived on either side of us walked with us. I felt protected when walking with those big 8th grade boys!

I remember getting sick in the first grade. Of course, there was no phone to call my parents to come get me. So, one of those big boys took me home on his sled. After that long, slow ride home, my mother tucked me in to bed, but not before I was given a dose of castor oil! That seemed to be a general cure-all for colds and flu. It was very unpleasant.

The main game that was played in the schools was baseball. I remember the rules used to be that we couldn't choose sides or play ball on teams. That would be too similar to the worldly way. When I was in the upper grades we often chose sides, in spite of the rules. I doubt that the rule is being enforced anymore, in that community.

We also played "Anti-over", "23-exidee", and "New Orleans", and when there was snow, it was "Fox and Geese", or similar games. On rainy days, we played "Upset the Fruit Basket", "I Spy", or "Dollar, Dollar". In "Dollar, Dollar", we gathered in a circle, and a silver dollar was passed from hand to hand. One person stood in the middle and had to guess where the silver dollar was. As soon as they guessed the right person, the culprit had to get into the middle.

I was about nine years old when the mocking started in school. This included making rude and degrading remarks and whispering. Often, the other children made fun of me for being the "Teacher's Pet." Things that I didn't understand were going on in church and some of the parents were mad at my dad. So, I guess that hatred the school children heard from their parents was directed at me.

The worst part was that the non-Amish teacher we had at the time, heard about all this, and turned against me, too. The next teacher I had was very good to me and took my side. By then, I had contracted a mysterious illness and missed a lot of school. I also had emotional problems during my illness. I would cry for hours and nobody could stop me. I felt so sick and weak physically and the mocking took a big toll on me. Thinking back, I realize I actually felt suicidal. It would have helped if my parents had held me and told me they loved me, but Amish parents normally do not show many signs of affection and give very little or no praise at all.

Anyway, my dad took me to many different doctors and they were all puzzled. I ran a slight temperature for four years. I also had a sore throat most of the time, was extremely tired, and I would often be in bed for weeks at a time with flu-like symptoms. At age 11, they took my tonsils out and I almost bled to death. The doctors put me to sleep again and did things to try to stop the bleeding.

When my dad was giving blood for me, he heard the nurses call out, "Code Blue!" Later, my dad told me he was sure he'd lost me, but somehow, I pulled through.

Shortly thereafter, our family doctor said he wanted to test me for something. He said the night before he had been looking through some old medical books for a clue to my illness. Yes, he said, it was undulant fever and that it caused thin blood. A blood test was taken that proved it. That also explained the excessive, heavy bleeding when I had my periods. An

Amish couple from Missouri visited us one day and she had had the illness, too. She told us how she was cured by a doctor in Kansas City, Kansas...So my dad sent me by bus to Jasper, Kansas, where I stayed with some friends. Their girls used to be my classmates in Indiana. My dad hadn't been able to go with me, so someone else accompanied me.

My friends took me to Kansas City by train every week for six weeks, and I received two shots each time. The doctor there informed me that undulant fever comes from cows' milk, and that I also had lepto (leptospirosis), which causes cows to abort their calves. He told me that childbearing would be unbearable for me. Some things the doctor described proved to be exactly as he said.

Child-bearing would have been very difficult even if I had no work to do. However, the heavy workload on our Clinton farm made it worse.

The Amish and the Education System

The Amish don't get any education beyond the eighth grade, which is really all they need for their lifestyle. After they finish 8th grade, they are then taught how to do the things they have to do to live their lifestyle. The boys need to work with their fathers or older siblings to learn everything about farming or carpentry. Depending on the father's trade, they learn buggy building, harness making, or a similar trade. Occasionally, boys are hired out to other Amish farms, since they do not pursue higher education.

Girls learned cooking, baking, sewing, quilting and canning. They also learned how to catch and butcher roosters, which were often served at the noon meal in the summer time, when company came, or for the thrashers. Unlike modern girls who are taught to get a higher education, Amish girls often work at home...

Amish people are taught that children must not know anything about the "birds and the bees," so as I grew older things become more and more mysterious.

When I asked where babies come from or why a pregnant woman has such a big belly, adults just gave evasive answers.

I know in some families the younger ones learned forbidden things from older siblings, who had figured things out. Being around farm animals helped them understand some of the facts of life. Sometimes the older boys in school would pass on what they knew to the younger ones. I know this happened to my brothers when they huddled in the toilet on a rainy day. They couldn't contain their excitement and gave us girls enough hints that we figured out they had learned about a forbidden subject. They certainly didn't share it with us, though!

Poor me; I had only my imagination and observations, but slowly I figured some things out. I began to notice that a woman with a very big belly would stay out of church a few times, and then you heard the couple had a baby. They came back to church when the baby was four weeks old and lo and behold, that big belly was gone! I still had to figure out how the baby got there, and how in the world it got out.

I remember one day when I was 12 years old, my half-sister Anna, who was married, came to spend the day and I hoped I could get some details from her. So bit by bit I told her what I already knew. She would scold me, and ask, "Who told you?" Then I'd explain how I figured it out. She seemed to be horrified, but I kept on in a teasing way and pretended I knew more than I did, hoping this would cause her to drop some information that I desperately wanted to know.

Of course, it didn't work.

CHAPTER FIVE

Out-of-School

When I went back home from Kansas, I had never before felt so good in my whole life! My dad had his first heart attack the year before, in 1965, and while still in the hospital he had a second one that really damaged his heart. So, he was mostly in bed for a year.

Upon arriving at home, I went straight back to school and passed seventh and eighth grade in three months; thanks to a very good, certified, non-Amish teacher. He was from Germany, knew German very well, and taught us well. I have a little secret that the Amish don't know about. They don't want anybody to read the Bible in English, a language they can understand. Well, here's my secret: I understood German very well, too. I knew what I was saying when I sang those songs, and I memorized many verses. This probably made it easier to find the truth later on.

After I got back, my mother's health broke down from caring for dad so long. We also had many visitors which added to the work load. Because I was in school, we had a hired girl, but when I got home in the evenings I worked very hard. It was so fun to work and I also wanted to prove to everybody that I was not lazy!

Later that fall I got sick again, so the Kansas City doctor told us to come back for more shots, which I did.

He said I had the disease so long it weakened my glands and immune system. I was a little sickly off and on until I was 17. I had hepatitis B, bronchitis, etc., but I worked whenever I could.

Most of the sewing was done in the winter time and I loved to sew. When I was 15, I made six shirts in one day for my brothers. I remember my dad wrote that to his sister in Virginia. Also when I was 15, the neighbor lady (who had 11 children,) asked me to come over one day and make a corduroy winter coat for her husband. It was a challenge, but I did it.

That was also the time my mother taught me how to cook and bake. The men were putting up a hog house across the road and invited some neighbor men to help. My mother wanted to go to town and she thought it would be a good experience for me to plan and cook that meal all by myself. It was a little scary and all I remember about the meal is that two of the dishes were macaroni and raisin pudding.

Winters could be a bit boring sometimes, especially when we had to crack and pick out hickory nuts that we had gathered in the fall. A job I really hated was tearing up worn out clothes into about one and one half inch strips for carpet rags and sewing them together, then rolling them up in balls. Usually someone in the community had a carpet loom and they'd make carpets for us out of those strips.

CHAPTER SIX

Teen Years

The community celebrated three, two-day holidays. This happened on Christmas, Easter, and Pentecost. The young folks were allowed to spend the night with someone, which usually was a younger married couple. It wasn't as likely that a younger couple would tattle about things that went on. On the second day, the young folks were usually invited to someone's home for dinner; they called it a "crowd". A lot of beer was consumed on all those two-day holidays.

The Pentecost holiday was called *Pinksta*, (both Sunday and Monday), which meant lilacs. The lilac bushes were usually blooming at that time. On the calendar, it said Pentecost, but I don't believe very many people knew what it meant. To me, the meaning was very vague, but I figured it must mean something holy or we wouldn't have observed it.

It was on a *Pinkst* Monday that an incident happened just after our night together. I was really happy and felt naughty enough to wear some kind of cheap, plain ring on my finger that I'd found.

There were six of us couples who decided to go on a long ride out west of the community to see where some Amish people had lived years ago. Each couple had their own horse and open buggy and we were all traveling close behind each other. A brown paper bag blew in front of the first horse and he stopped dead in his tracks.

We were next in line and our horse ran into the buggy ahead of us. Our wheels locked and both of our buggies tipped on their sides. I was thrown out and slowly rolled down a very long, steep ditch. Our horse ran away with the buggy hitting him and cutting into his hind legs.

The buggies behind us couldn't stop either, and buggy numbers three, four, and five also rolled. Buggy number six was the only one left standing. I remember standing in that ditch looking up at that tangled mess, and being thankful that I hadn't died with that ring on my finger. I took it off right then and there! It seems I didn't get away with anything, did I?

My dad was always interested in what went on in the world, especially in regard to the presidents. He always knew which one he hoped would win in the election year. I think he got most of his information from talking to "Englishers".

It so happened that a few of us young folks were talking about a president and one of the boys said, "My dad doesn't think we should ask after the world. A good Christian doesn't do that." I guess their view or definition of the world was different, otherwise they could recognize that they already lived in the world and didn't have to point anywhere else. Anyway, I would get most of my information from scanning the front pages of newspapers in stores; I could read a page at a glance, and that's probably why I picked up more. Many of the "Englishers" in my life were amazed, and would ask me where I got all my information if I didn't have TV, radio, or daily papers.

One winter day when I was 18, my brothers brought the mail in. I stopped my sewing long enough to glance at the world news on the front page of Cappers Weekly. It named the new Miss America and gave her measurements. I grabbed the tape measure to find out if I possibly could be close. I was right on the dot, but it didn't impress me much at all and was soon forgotten.

I didn't walk and dress or have the posture of Miss America anyway, so nobody could have known. My dad also didn't like to see anyone looking in a mirror very long. We might have a little one on the medicine cabinet and some small ones in drawers to use when we got dressed. When my brother Joseph was about 10, he was on the porch looking in a window that had the curtain down, and it served as a mirror. He loved to watch himself as he made faces and did all kinds of crazy things in front of it. One day he got caught when dad discovered him, and that was the end of that!

One day when I was 16, I was wearing sun glasses while mowing the lawn. Joseph was 11 and he was standing waiting until I finished. He had one of my dad's big, wide-brimmed straw hats, and he wanted me to put it on. He had me pose in different ways and said I looked exactly like some models in a Sears's catalog who were modeling long dresses. It would not have been good if dad had caught us, and much worse if I had been standing in front of the window Joseph had used as a mirror!

Growing Pains

Just when I turned 17, my half-brother, Ben, and his wife, Ida, moved to another farm. Along with my parents, they decided my other brothers were old enough now to take over the farming. They were 15 and 16, and I think Ben had some misgivings about how it would go at milking time. If we did too much talking and laughing, or goofing off, then the cows wouldn't let down their milk, and it would hurt the production. We were always playing jokes on each other.

My brother Atlee was so gullible that it was pretty easy to fool him, and we sure got some good ones on him! He and Marvin were inseparable when growing up. Atlee was the leader and Marvin the follower. If Atlee was bad, Marvin was bad, and vice-versa. Malinda had natural curls and always had one curl in the middle of her forehead, so her nickname was Curly.

Joseph was quieter and very intelligent. I was amazed when I taught him in 8th grade, and at the conversations we had on the way home from school. Dora was my adorable baby sister who had a knack for staying out of trouble.

When my brothers became 17 they had a hard time proving themselves, and at first the other boys threatened to knock them out. So you can imagine what they had to do to survive!

That last year at home was miserable, especially for my parents. Family life as we had known it ceased to exist. Mealtimes were not peaceful, because my dad would always be warning and preaching to get the boys to change. It fell on deaf ears, but I took it all in. It filled me with dread and fear and often I'd go away from the table and sit in the outhouse, until I thought they were about finished eating.

More before Marriage Memories

One memory was about an incident that happened when I was 15 years old. I endured an isolated mocking from a group of six young folks, led by a girl. There were three boys and three girls. When I walked past this group, they laughed uncontrollably. I knew they were laughing at me because there was nobody else around. It just took away any self-esteem or confidence that I had.

When I was very close to 17, I was in church in another district and after services we girls were upstairs in the back room, when I heard some boys enter the front room. Soon the girls needed to go downstairs and we had to pass through that room. I was terrified, because some of the wilder boys were there, too. Since I was the youngest, I was last. Sure enough, as I passed them there were whistles. I felt my insides shrivel because I thought they were mocking me. I guess that's what I expected.

Aaron had been there, too. Later, I asked him about it and he assured me that nobody had been mocking me; they whistled because I was beautiful. It took me awhile to digest that one and turn it around. My confidence began to build as I got older. Aaron would also tell me what people said, like when he took me to meet his "English" neighbors, how they had a fit and said I was the most beautiful turtledove they ever saw. Teaching school helped, too, especially when I'd hear through a friend that somebody thought I was doing a good job.

Unfortunately, it didn't take long for a budding, confident personality to change to an inhibited and withdrawn one after marriage. Nothing about it makes any sense.

I had a close friend, Amelia Beachy, who would tell me things that others said, too. The years between 14 and 17 could be a boring time, to be out of school and not yet with the youth. So, Amelia and I would go to see a neighbor, Rachel Helmuth, on Sunday afternoons and play games like "Life", "Sorry", "Monopoly", etc.

Amelia and I sat beside each other in church. At age twelve we started sitting with the girls, instead of sitting with the mothers. She and I did a lot of whispering during church time, which we could hide pretty well, because the girls usually sat on the very back bench. The bench in front of us was for the boy's, who came in at the last minute at 9 o'clock. The men sat in front of the boys and the women sat in the kitchen facing the men.

The congregation knelt in prayer facing the back. Imagine how embarrassing it was with those boys kneeling behind us. Sometimes they'd pester us by tugging on our apron belts or cape corners, etc. It didn't happen often to me, but they loved to tease Rachel. Usually she could take care of herself and the boys didn't get the best of her.

On one particular day they were especially mean and by the time you looked around to see who it was, their heads were down like they were praying to Almighty God.

When we got up from praying, some Scriptures were read while we stood. I bet Rachel couldn't wait until we sat down again. She was a dwarf, but I can still see her take out a straight pin from her cape and jab it deep into one of the boys' behinds. It was such satisfaction to see that look of shock and pain on his face and I was surprised that he didn't let out a yelp!

When I turned the scary age of 17; I was on the threshold of getting ready to court. That's one thing that worried me.

Dating and Courtship Rituals

Since I was 15, I had dreaded the time when I'd turn 17 and be joining the young folks. I would often go back to the woods and cry. I so wished my parents would move to a community where the young folks weren't so bad. It was extra hard for me because I had no older siblings that were or had been with the young folks. I had so many questions; I had never been in a singing.

A singing is where the young folks get together on Sunday evenings to sing German songs. They are allowed to sing faster tunes than the very slow songs that are sung in church services. This is where the boys ask the girls for dates, to take place after they finish singing. Teenagers start going to singings at age 17, and not one day sooner.

I knew that the rules for dating were that the couple had to sit on a rocking chair, with the boy holding the girl on his lap. This was such a crazy rule; it is a tradition that has been handed down for generations. I didn't think anyone would ask me for a date, but I desperately wanted to know what took place, just in case. I was terrified that I'd do something stupid, and I didn't want to ask anyone, afraid they'd know what

I was thinking. What a predicament! I found out that hardly anybody used the rocking chair anymore. Most couples thought that outdated, so they were sitting or lying down on the couch with their dates.

When my dad found out about that, he consulted another bishop and was advised to put the couch in my parents' bedroom! Now what? Well, I got a big comforter and some covers and stuffed them in a small closet under the stairs, before I went to the singing. The singing was in a different district of the community, about 12 miles away.

I was just flabbergasted to see that some of the girls had been drinking. Many of the bishops or ministers' children thought they had to be extra bad to prove that they wouldn't tattle. Tattling was a severe no-no if you wanted to survive. I felt a lot of peer pressure, but they didn't judge me as someone who would tattle as long as they hadn't caught me. After the singing, I heard the boys trying to talk Aaron into asking me for a date. When Aaron agreed, the boy told his girlfriend. She asked me for Aaron. My answer was, "Yes".

How I dreaded it, because I was sure I'd do something stupid. My neighbor, little Rachel, hitched a ride home with us. She and I sat on the narrow seat and Aaron sat on my lap. Then, something unexpected happened. He turned half-way around and put his arm around me! Oh, my! How embarrassing!

That was a long ride home. Aaron drove the horse with one hand. We got home about midnight and he put the horse in the barn. When we went in the house, sure enough, the couch was missing. Dad had moved it into the bedroom! I quickly dug out that bedding and made a nest on the floor, while Aaron took off his coat and hat, and lo and behold, his shoes, jacket and suspenders! I took off my cap and glasses and later learned you also take off the cape and apron. That prevents the boy from getting stuck with pins when he holds you tight.

I soon sensed that Aaron felt right at home and I hadn't done anything too dumb, so we had a nice visit until 2 a.m. That's the time the rules say the boys have to go home. My dad would knock on the door if he didn't leave at that time.

It took a while to figure out if I was expected to put my arm around the boy, too. I was on the lookout to see how other couples did it. I wasn't sure if this was just some crazy thing the boys did, and I sure didn't want to be caught doing so until I knew for sure! Finally, on Easter Sunday, I saw other girls doing it, so I conjured up the nerve that night on my fifth date - with one of the other guys. Hadn't I come a long way?

Couch Situation

What happened with the couch situation? I don't remember how it all came about, but I had some extremely curious siblings, and one of them decided to check that little closet, and told mom to come look. Well, I had a good talk with my parents and got them to see my point of view. I replaced the "nest" with the couch. The "couch" was just a folding cot that could be adjusted so one end stayed up. This made it necessary to be in a sitting position. I explained that sitting side by side on that cot was much better than the floor or the rocking chair! It worked. That old cot stayed in the living room and I kept my promise to keep the head up.

I did a naughty thing on my second date with Aaron. I got out a cigar box I had discovered that held my dad's notes about church matters. There was some information about some of the boys who were members of our church. They had been seen here or there doing bad things or someone had tattled to the ministers. That was really exciting to Aaron and I was shocked when later he said he had told the other boys, and they would pay me $20 if I brought those notes to the singing.

Wow, did my conscience struggle with that one! It was almost like, "make it or break it", for survival, and finally I did it. I think it helped to assure them that I wasn't a tattler. I have no idea if my dad ever missed the notes, but those boys could now outsmart the ministers. I also broke small little rules with dress, if it was something everyone else did, but I never smoked or drank. I had a friend, Ruth Miller, the deacon's daughter, who didn't smoke or drink either, and we helped each other stick it out.

When I was 18 years old, I was asked to teach school and I said I'd try. I had 18 pupils from first to eighth grade. My brother, Joseph, was in the 8th grade and my sister, Dora, was in the 5th grade.

The distance was one and a half miles to school, so my two siblings and I went by horse and buggy. This horse was an all-purpose horse and she was ever so slow! Her name was Maple. She took such short little steps, and when we poked her with a stick, she'd speed up for about six steps. It sure took patience! That was a healthier year for me, being outdoors much more, and feeling very good about being given the responsibility of teaching, too.

It really was a challenge because they had some poor teachers before me. Many times I felt like giving up, and I also had a problem family. Our neighbor, Roman Helmuth, was on the school board. After questioning me, the board decided I needed a strap to whip the misbehaving children. The board members told the parents that's what I would do, since apparently they couldn't control them. Well, I couldn't make myself use it, but the boys did turn out okay without it.

I never could chop off a rooster's head either! There were times when no one else was around when I needed one. I'd think, "This time I'm doing it!" I'd catch one and get his head between the two nails on the chunk of wood, and lift the hatchet, but to this day I've never done it. I suppose the roosters would say it turned out okay for them, too, for awhile anyway!

On picnic day, the school board asked me to teach again the next term, but I had wedding plans.

CHAPTER SEVEN

Courtship and Wedding

Sometimes, courting evenings could become very challenging! In the communities, we had what we called "up-cutters". They were a bunch of single boys who loved to call on couples who were dating. They wanted to disturb the evening for the couple. In earlier years, it had started as just a lot of fun, but it had turned into something bad. The boys were now destroying property and food and made big messes throughout the house. On one occasion, they dumped a big wastebasket full of trash on our heads! We were fortunate to live on the far end of the community, so because of the distance they didn't come often. It got so out of hand that newly formed communities would put in their rules, "no up-cutting".

Following a two year courtship, Aaron asked me to marry him in the spring of 1971. His mother wanted to sell her farm that fall and it was expected that he would buy it. I guess he thought he needed a wife to help him. In the Amish culture there are no engagement or wedding rings and no one except the immediate family finds out about the engagement, until two or three weeks before the wedding. That's when the bishop announces it in church. Aaron lived with us during those two weeks to help with the wedding preparations. We were married in September of 1971, when I was 19 years old and Aaron was 21. I was a virgin, but not all of the girls were. There were pregnant girls who had to get married in our community, just like in the world.

I remember when my dad performed our wedding ceremony. He was so overcome that he almost couldn't get it done. He would just break down and cry. Maybe he shared my forebodings, I don't know. I think my dad noticed that I was hurt and sad during the time Aaron stayed with us for the wedding preparations.

It was warm enough that the service could be held in a machine shed. Otherwise, it would have to take place in a neighbor's house. The home of the bride's family was set up with tables and lots of borrowed dishes. About 20 cooks, mainly relatives and neighbors, were preparing the big meal.

There were also four to six couples serving as table waiters. Some were steady couples and other pairs consisted of relatives from both sides and our friends.

The wedding ceremony was very similar to a regular church service. The bride and groom sat on a separate bench with another couple seated on each side of them as their witnesses. My brother Atlee and Aaron's sister Erma, his sister Wilma and her boyfriend Elmer, witnessed us. When the singing began the ministers stepped aside, as they normally do. The wedding couple followed and sat on a bench facing the ministers while they are given advice and admonishments about marriage. When we were dismissed and went back to the shed, the six of us now sat on special chairs that faced each other, not far from the preacher. The bishop would then conduct the marriage ceremony toward the end of the sermon. After the services were almost over, the six of us went to the house where the reception was being held. We sat around a corner of the table near the big wedding cake and giant bowl of fruit. When the guests were all seated and eating, our food was given to us in special dishes. Some of the food was "special ordered" which really made us feel special.

The evening of our wedding some bad things happened after the boys discovered their beer had been stolen from the back of their buggies. Some ex-Amish boys arrived and were blamed for the theft. They denied it and a fight began. There were a lot of threats at first, like "Your heads are going to go flying over the barn" and similar remarks to each other. Before it was over most of the wedding guests were outside watching the fight. One of the neighbor boys was beaten up and his nose was broken. That incident sure spoiled the celebration for everyone that night.

The Amish don't have honeymoons, so the newlyweds stay at home to help clean up the mess, and return borrowed dishes. The two couples who sat with us as witnesses, also stayed to help the next day. The tons of dishes from the night before hadn't been washed, so the tables were exactly as they had been after the guests went home.

We moved to Aaron's farm which he had been farming since his dad died when Aaron was 14. His dad had also been a bishop before he died.

My mother-in-law, Barbara, was left with her four daughters, and Aaron. The girls helped Aaron with the farming. Susie and Naomi had already been married, when we moved to the farm. When Wilma married shortly afterward, Barbara and Erma moved into the little house which was right across from ours, separated by a gravel lane between the two houses. The five older brothers, Samuel, Edwin, Jacob, Ervin, and Alvin, had left home and were married. The last three brothers had left the Amish years ago.

This farm was 10 miles from my family's home so we didn't go back and forth very often. When I'd want to go see my family for the day, often the answer was some excuse about the horse; he needed to be shod, or lost a shoe, or had too long of a trip recently.

CHAPTER EIGHT

Marriage Woes in the Early Years

Let me see if I can write a few things about my marriage woes. I compare my marriage to a small boy trying to hold a cute little orange kitty. He loves it, but has no idea how to hold it. He squeezes and hurts the little thing and is surprised to hear it squeal and meow, and then squeezes harder. An adult takes it away before it gets killed, until the little boy grows up more. Well, this little boy didn't grow up, and nobody took away the little kitty, in my case.

Thank God, it's safe now. There is too much to tell every detail, but I want to share some incidents.

We moved into the little house on his mom's farm two weeks after we were married. We exchanged houses with her a year later. Anyway, I guess my expectations were too high.

A friend, who had been married for a year before us, told me how wonderful marriage was and how her husband held her in his arms all night long. So, here I was a young bride who needed some comfort in this strange environment away from home. After we got in bed, I tried to snuggle up to Aaron, but he pushed me away.

"I'm not used to anyone sleeping with me and I don't want anyone against me," Aaron said brusquely.

Well, I cried silently without ceasing all night long. He woke up several times and caught me crying. Instead of comforting me, he'd grunt in a very irritated voice, "Ahhh, what's wrong with you?" Then he'd go right back to sleep.

Among other things, my parents gave us a cow and a young heifer from their herd for a wedding gift. We could choose any cow we wanted, so I picked Stina because she was extra-large and was an easy milker.

Aaron's cows were small Guernsey's and Stina looked like Goliath beside them.

One day in the first week after we moved to the farm, while I was ironing, Aaron told me to come help him get my cows back in. They had broken through a fence in the pasture. I tried my best to help, but his anger was directed at me, too. I was never at the right place, at the right time, no matter how hard I tried. I hadn't realized before then that I was so dumb and stupid! He fixed the fence, but before long it happened again.

I was a wreck by the time it stopped. One night, I had finished milking and was ready to go in and make supper, when Aaron asked me to go light a lantern, then bring it out to the barn.

When I got back to the barn, I saw a horrifying sight. My Stina had tried to break out or something, and for revenge he had her head in a stanchion, which is how a cow is tied up while being milked. He was trying to force her to go through something which was meant only for the head. Apparently, Stina was upset about being in strange surroundings.

"Go through that stanchion!" he ordered Stina, as if she could understand. Aaron began poking her with a pitch fork. Sometimes he used a hammer, too. Meantime, she was down on her front knees and bellowing. Stina's eyes were swollen and she had other injuries. I stood there, helpless, wringing my hands, and making an "uh uh" sound.

Then, Aaron angrily turned to me. "Get to the house," he barked. My heart was already breaking. Even now, I can see my heart on the ground outside that barn, shattered like glass in thousands of pieces. I had choked back my tears before he came in to eat

I learned very quickly that Aaron hated tears. After all, crying wouldn't be making him happy.

This became a pattern. I could never talk to him or anyone about the verbal abuse that began to happen. There was really no one to go to. The family system is set up with the husband having all the power, and outsiders cannot interfere.

The First Summer

Aaron's family couldn't understand that I wasn't as strong as they were. My childhood illnesses had left my immune and glandular systems weakened.

There was a grove of trees behind the house and those leaves blew all over the giant lawn. Some of the family got together to rake it all in one day. I tried to keep up non-stop with the rest.

We finished that evening with 15 manure spreader loads of damp, packed leaves, and when I went in the house I totally collapsed and fainted just as I hit the bed. It took me days to recover. My muscles were so sore I could hardly move. Another time I tried husking corn for a whole day. Aaron's sister also helped and I couldn't do that either. I wanted to, so badly. It seemed like my worth as an in-law and wife diminished drastically.

The next summer was very hard because I was pregnant and had many difficulties. I had to mow that giant lawn every week, plus keep the big garden clean, do all the canning, the milking, and other chores Aaron assigned to me.

One day when I was mowing the lawn, a salesman or somebody stopped beside me on his way up to the house to see Aaron's mom. He pointed to where Aaron stood visiting with a feed salesman and asked me, "Why isn't that guy mowing the lawn?" He seemed almost angry that this pregnant woman had to do it.

So later, I asked Aaron why he doesn't have time to help me if he can visit with salesmen for three hours. His answer was, "That's something I enjoy doing," like I should be able to understand that. I also learned that summer when I wanted to tell him how tired I was or how much I hurt, it was like talking to the wind.

A few incidents still stand out in my memory from that first summer. I always went to town with fear that I'd get some groceries that his family didn't buy. That was a big crime you didn't want to commit. They bought things that our family didn't buy either. I would have to report what was spent in every store, down to the penny so Aaron could write it down. I loved ice cream and I would long for a cone or a bar, but didn't dare spend the money for it.

At 14, my dad had trusted me to go to town to buy groceries and I bought ice cream without thinking twice. One particular time Aaron's mom had come over, and he made me give him a report of how the money was spent from that day in town. I had lost the slip for the 5 and 10 cent store and couldn't remember the exact amount. I said it was somewhere between three and four dollars. He got very angry and chewed me out and oh, the horror that I felt when he did it in front of his mom! This was one of several times when she really defended me and told him what he did was very wrong.

Sometimes we would drive about nine miles to Orville with the horse and buggy. One morning we were going down the lane really fast. I cringed at the way the horse was being treated, and also that Aaron had no caring thought or mercy for his pregnant wife when going over the bumps at that speed. At some point along the way, he realized he had forgotten his billfold. He started raving angrily and blamed me because I hadn't kept him from forgetting!

One thing I always did was try to please him. Many days my heart would ache so badly. I not only didn't tell anyone about how I felt, I couldn't talk to Aaron, either.

CHAPTER NINE

More of the Early Years

Another incident happened about two and a half months before Betty was born. The oat bundles out in the field had to be gathered up and set on piles to dry out for thrashing. I wasn't able to help, so Aaron asked a neighbor and his sister Erma, who still lived at home, to help him. I was canning applesauce that day, which is very hard for a person to do alone. Then I had to cook a big meal for everyone who had been shocking oats. I used of lot of drinking water that day, which had to be carried from a well far up the hill. Usually, I kept two pails of water by the sink. One pail was the drinking water and the other was used for cleaning purposes. That water came from a well closer to the house. Carrying the well water took a lot of my energy that day, and I was very tired.
Well, when Aaron came in for dinner with his two helpers, I was already dishing out the food. He

discovered the pails of wash water were empty, and the workers could not wash their hands. It had slipped my mind because I was so busy and so tired. I was ready to drop! My husband started hammering me with accusations. He couldn't ever seem to stop at one cutting or hurtful remark; he would go on and on.

I was so horrified about what my neighbors must have thought of me, that I didn't know what to do. For me, it was such an unspeakable shame that Aaron thought I was a lousy wife. Erma then helped dish out the food while the men waited until I brought in the water. I also had to get drinking water and I'll never forget how heavy those pails were!

I still had more apples to put through a cone shaped machine for making apple sauce. The work table was loaded with dishes after we were done eating. To my great surprise, Erma offered to help with that giant pile of dishes. She told me in a lighthearted way,

"Don't take things that Aaron says so seriously. That's just the way he is." I felt like saying, "Yeah, tell me when it's too late!"

I'm going to share one more thing that happened that summer which shocked me and turned out to become normal for the rest of our married life. I had been longing to go visit my half-brother, Ben, and his wife, Ida, one evening and surprise them with a freezer of homemade ice cream. So, one morning at the breakfast table, I talked it over with Aaron and he agreed. We even discussed that he might be coming home late that evening so I could bring the horse, Zedar, in from the pasture for him. It seemed like a normal conversation.

So, that evening after I had the freezer on the buggy, Aaron came home as I was bringing the horse in. He asked me, "Why in the world are you doing that?"

I told him and then asked, "Don't you remember what we talked about this morning?" He acted very surprised. "I never said anything like that."

We did end up going to Ben's house, but the fun was zapped out of the evening. I could rarely have real conversations at the table because Aaron never really saw or heard me.

One thing he did notice was when the food wasn't on the table instantly.

Sometimes he would explain how his mind was just too full with work, business, and all, and it just couldn't hold everything. He would say he only allowed the important things in his mind. That didn't do anything for my feelings! I have learned since that time, it's one of the traits of a controller.

I've been avoiding the next subject, which happened after Betty's birth. It is so painful to think about, I just start crying.

CHAPTER TEN

New Baby Woes

My oldest child was a little girl named Betty, born in October, 1972. As traumatic as her birth was, I never even tried to describe it when other women were talking about their experiences. There just weren't any words.

My doctor could've prevented a lot of my suffering if he had heeded the nurses' calls during the last few hours of my labor. I guess he needed to finish up with the patients in his office first. I was sent home the next day and I remember being so weak that when I walked into the house the walls looked tilted and the floors came up. Fortunately, it wasn't far to the bed. Due to severe pain from complications and caring for my newborn baby, I didn't get the rest I needed that first week.

Amish women were taught to stay in bed for 10 days.

This gave them time to rest and also prevented them from doing the hard work too soon. For many this was hard to do when they felt well enough to be up. I certainly had no problem that way. Because I hadn't been able to fully relax since giving birth I was not getting the rest I desperately needed.

Around the fifth night, being physically and emotionally exhausted, I dozed off. While I was sleeping, I had a vivid dream of being in a boat and rowing over to the other side of a lake. Just before reaching the shore, I woke up; I was hardly able to breathe. I felt like I was losing consciousness. A dark feeling washed over me in waves. Aaron and his mom were really scared because I was so pale. They went to the neighbor's house and called the ambulance which took me to the hospital.

After my admission, the doctor said I'd gone home too soon and needed a lot of rest. After being relieved of the discomforts of severe constipation and having the stitches tended to, I was finally able to relax a bit.

The memory that is still painfully vivid is when Anna, my half-sister, came with Aaron to visit me while I was in the hospital. I was telling her about the heavy work load I had before the baby came and how impossible it would be to continue that way now with the baby to care for. I explained to her that many times I wasn't able to run to the outhouse because I barely had enough time to get breakfast ready.

Then Aaron leaned forward, put his arm on my shoulder and so tenderly and lovingly said, "You know, you don't have to do all that."

Now Anna was impressed and I was left with such awful shock and surprise at his deceit!

After I got back home, the weather was turning colder. We had to get the wood stove going and keeping it going was usually my job. I was concerned about how I would be able to lift the heavy pail of coal and heavy pieces of wood. The hired girl took care of keeping the stove going during the day, but it was up to me during the night.

We had put the crib in the living room where it would be warmer for the baby. One night when she was about two weeks old, she woke me up wanting to be fed. It was after midnight. The fire had gone out so it was cold in the house. The baby wasn't just hungry. She was also cold and I wanted to nurse her right away.

I tried so hard to wake Aaron up to attend to the stove, but he wouldn't get up. He would rouse and answer me, then groan and go back to sleep. Finally, I nursed her anyway, which was very miserable because the house was so cold. In a short time, I had a raging breast infection from getting chilled!

The milk gave the baby a bellyache that turned into the colic and she screamed for months. I couldn't find any milk that agreed with her and finally, when she was 6 months old, we got a goat. Thankfully, the goat milk worked for her.

More Baby Woes

Baby Betty was 2 months old when Aaron's sister, Erma, married Amos Shetler. Since she lived with her mom in the little house, the wedding had to be held in our bigger house. The baby was still screaming a lot. I remember hearing some older women talking in church and they were declaring that something must be wrong with that baby!

Betty screamed whenever I gave her a bath. I had noticed a big black and blue spot near the sacrum area. So I took her to the doctor to have him look at it. He said there was nothing wrong, but some years later we found out that if he had taken an X-ray it would have shown a broken tail bone, which occurred at birth.

During the week before the wedding, we had to sleep in the other house so we could set up the tables in our house. More and more of Aaron's family kept arriving, as well as from the groom's family. It was a stressful time and with all the damage done from the emotional abuse, I was feeling very inferior to Aaron's family. So the next episode was extremely painful.

One evening the living room was full of relatives when my baby started to scream again. I went into the bedroom and tried my best to quiet her. After awhile I got so tired, I wished my husband or someone would take a turn. Instead, he came in and commanded, "Shut her up! Shut that baby up! What do you think they're all thinking out there? The only reason she's screaming is because you're nervous and she feels that." That was when I realized he saw the baby and me as a big embarrassment to his family. I'll never forget the deep pain and heavy feeling in my heart whenever I woke up during that night. All I could do at the time was to accept the fact and go on, hoping I could please him someday if I just tried harder.

When the baby was three months old, she didn't cry for longer periods. I remember going to an Amish farm sale one cold day and I enjoyed it, that is—until it got really late and Aaron was not ready to go home yet. Now I would have to do all the many house chores before the milking, in the dark. It was so cold. I was already really cold from the buggy ride home, and then I had to be outside for another few hours!

Often the house was cold until the stove got fired up again. I had to go so far to get the wood, so I used a big box with sled runners underneath. It was very heavy and hard to pull, but doing it that way I only had to make one trip out to the wood pile. Afterward,

I experienced a lot of pain in my shoulder and later found out I had a torn muscle.

Then, when the baby was four months old, we were going to my parents' home for the evening. The baby was all bundled up when she started to scream again. Usually, the buggy ride would put her to sleep, but it didn't work this time.

Aaron's anger had gotten worse and he shouted at me, "Shut her up!" I couldn't settle Betty down. All of a sudden, he put the reins to the horse between his legs, then grabbed the baby out of my lap and slapped her little face, again and again, until his anger subsided a bit. I don't remember how long she cried. I cried, too, only my sobs stayed on the inside. I was so shocked, I was numb.

Sadly, my family didn't detect that anything was wrong. My sisters say now I really put up a good front to hide it all. Later, I found out this was typical of battered woman syndrome.

CHAPTER ELEVEN

More Indiana Stories

I think I probably became numb to the abuse after that first year and a half. But, I still have some memories from the next few years before we moved to Clinton, Michigan. One memory that stands out happened on a day we went to my parents' home to help my family butcher a cow.

It must have been in January because it was way below zero when we started on that long ride home. It would take at least an hour and I dreaded it so much. I knew how cold my hands and feet usually got, and we couldn't have "storm fronts" on the buggy in that community.

Sometimes I used a blanket to try and protect my face. I was also holding 15 month old Betty who was all bundled up and heavy to hold for that long.

Because it was so late, I knew what lay ahead when we got home still having all the chores to do. The house would be cold, and the coal smoke from the stove made me sick. When we had gone about four miles, Aaron wanted to stop at the Amish harness shop to buy something. Aaron didn't want to have to bundle us up again, so he told me to stay in the buggy. I groaned on the inside and asked him to please make it quick, that I was already cold.

I could peek out of the tiny buggy window and see him through the shop window. It didn't take long to make the purchase, but then he and the shop owner stood there for the longest time visiting. I could see them doubling over with laughter, while I sat there shivering, getting colder and colder.

Little Betty was getting fussy, too, and it seemed like a very, very, long time before Aaron finally came out. I was stomping my feet to keep them from becoming numb, and we still had six miles to go!

I didn't say anything when he finally came out to the buggy, but I felt such injustice since he could never wait more than a minute for me. So sometime later, when his mood seemed to be good, I wanted to talk to him in a nice way to see if he would understand what I had suffered and how it wasn't right.

It turned out that the only thing he could understand was that he enjoyed visiting and there was nothing wrong with that. So, instead of getting some understanding and even a little compassion that would help me feel better, my heart just ached that much more.

The thought of a whole lifetime like this ahead of us was really scary and filled me with dread!

There was more heartbreaking abuse with little Betty when he tried to train her with the whip method like he used with his horses. He had his animals so under control, he could call the horses by saying the word,

"Come." It appeared that he wanted to do the same with Betty, but she was terrified of him. He wouldn't allow me to pick her up to comfort her after he would spank her, and she was not yet two years old. I couldn't say a word as I looked on helplessly, my heart just silently screaming. I was thankful when Aaron no longer abused the babies in that way.

Betty was almost two when Alfred was born in 1974. He was a good baby, so happy and bright, until he was ten months old. He drank some kerosene he had found. It was a very hot day; I was in the garden picking green beans to can, and I often looked through the window to check on him. Betty was taking a nap, but Alfred couldn't settle down that day. He was crawling flat on his stomach and got into everything.

He had opened a little door behind the kitchen stove and taken everything out including a little tin can that held some kerosene that I had used the winter before to start the fire in the stove. I had no idea it was still there.

When I saw him lying on the floor, I first thought, "He's finally sleeping". Then I noticed a wet streak behind him on the floor, so I went in to check it out. I smelled the kerosene! He was barely breathing and was turning blue. I was terrified! I picked Alfred up in my arms and ran out to Aaron. The pony happened to be tied to the hitching post so Aaron was able to reach the "English" neighbor's house in a jiffy. The neighbor came right away and took us in his car at high speed to the emergency room. It helped Alfred's breathing some to keep his head by the open window. At the hospital, they pumped his stomach and kept him for two days to prevent pneumonia. The kerosene seriously damaged the lining or something vital in his intestines. Afterward, he had diarrhea and digestive problems; was pale, skinny, whiny, and didn't feel well. He finally recovered when he was two years old and was back to his old self.

The same thing happened to someone else in the community shortly after that.

More about Indiana

I had not complained to my parents about having to mow the huge lawn. The summer after Betty was born I was very thankful that they stepped in and said there was no way I was going to mow that big lawn again. My mother seemed really upset about it and without asking anybody's opinion she asked a single girl, Verna Yoder, who was a little older than me, to mow the lawn that summer.

Verna had to drive about six miles. I think my parents paid her. For the next few years our neighbors, the Millers, were kind enough to send their children over to mow our lawn, after doing their own chores. The oldest girl was probably in her early teens. The five oldest children could mow. We owned several push mowers and made sure we always had five in running order. I really enjoyed those children. They were well mannered and worked hard.

I don't remember what we paid them, but I usually had a bag of candy for them, after they were done. It was fun to watch them gather around that bag and take out their share, like they had been living for that moment all evening. I did, occasionally, mow the lawn when they couldn't, and I know I did it again the summer I was pregnant with Lorene. I had to take short breaks and sat on the lawn to rest a bit. I'd read the paper called Capper's Weekly that I enjoyed so much. I always saved it for those times.

We weren't allowed to get a daily paper, so I just devoured the weekly. There was a column on the front page that said "World News" and I really kept up with that bit of information.

As the years went by, I had become accustomed to my surroundings and our neighborhood, and of course, I had my little children to focus on. Playing games with my siblings down home, or having a picnic with Aaron's family gave me some better memories

In the summer of 1976, my dad started talking about moving to Clinton, Michigan. We were interested in moving with them.

It seemed everything was under control in that community with the young folks, and it looked like nobody broke the rules as far as dress was concerned.

In Butler County, the bad things going on among the youth had really spread like wildfire into the schools and I didn't want my children around bad influences.

I learned there were other bad influences in Clinton which were very different from the ones in Butler County. I noticed a self-righteous and extremely superior attitude regarding other communities that had problems or dressed in a more liberal way. The only way my girls would ever "belong" would be if they developed the same attitude, copied the same stiff postures, and looked down their noses (literally) like the other girls.

Between the two places, each with its own bad influences, I personally don't think there's much difference in God's eyes. At that time, there weren't many communities to choose from. In the next few years, many new ones were constantly popping up, especially in Wisconsin and the Midwest.

CHAPTER TWELVE

Move to Clinton, Michigan

Baby Lorene was born in 1977 and was only five weeks old when we moved to Clinton, Michigan. My parents and brothers and sisters came along to help unload the truck. My dad died less than three months later, before my parents could get moved. I would not have wanted to move if I thought my parents weren't going to move with us. So, it was especially hard to endure all the things we encountered in that community. I'm glad God knows everything that happened.

We had a lot of stuff because we didn't have a farm sale like most people did. We took 25 sows about ready to farrow (have their litter) and many half-grown feeder pigs, and all of our cows and heifers.

We had bought the farm in October, 1976 and moved in March, 1977. No words could express our shock to find out the owner hadn't hauled the manure all winter! He said his manure spreader broke and he had back problems. Well, he also had two big boys. Anyway, the pigs had to be put in the hog house in manure a foot deep or more, for the time being. There was also a big pile of manure in front of the barn, put there by a manual litter carrier. This is a large bucket that is pushed along a steel track. This track is attached to a beam and held up by sturdy posts. The track goes inside the barn and the bucket is then lowered by pulleys and filled with manure. Then, it is pulled up and pushed outside along that track, and dumped on a pile.

Aaron hauled about 50 spreader loads, done by hand with a pitchfork, after the manure thawed out. I could go on and on, but will skip to other things. The owners moved up the road about two miles, and remained one of our neighbors for the 11 years we lived there. Their names were Dan A. and Martha Mast. Our closest neighbors were Mose and Ida Schmucker who moved in from New York.

Most people from the East were well accepted, but most coming from Butler County, were considered scum, especially if they were young. Our neighbors were held in high esteem while we were treated like ex-convicts being watched for a misstep. It seemed they feared that we might bring the bad things from Butler County and contaminate their community. The bishop who held such control over most of the Midwest communities was Abe Stutzman. One of his ministers was Atlee Kurtz.

Later, in 1977, a family from Ohio moved in. The husband was a minister and later when the church was divided he was ordained bishop. He was my dad's double cousin and he reminded me much of my dad. I am grateful to him for making life a bit more tolerable. His name was Abner Gingerich.

After a very difficult pregnancy, our son Ivan was born in 1979. Doctors said, "You cannot have children anymore and you need to have a tubal ligation done."

To my chagrin, Aaron asked Bishop Abe Stutzman; so the ministers debated, and the verdict was, no. As a result, they got to watch me struggle through three more pregnancies in untold agony, with serious complications afterward. Plus the workload was more than most strong women could have handled. I will be forever grateful to a precious girl who decided to work for us after Ivan was born. Her name was Emma Raber. Emma's sister Katie helped us, too. It took me a long time to recover from that pregnancy.

Miriam was born at home in 1981. Because Emma was helping me, things went better this time. Emma went home when Miriam was just four weeks old. Marilyn was born in 1982, and David was born in 1985. And that's it!

When David was a year old, I started a bakery in my home to help save the farm. We had been struggling for several years to keep up with the interest we owed on the debt we had from buying the farm. So we did everything we could think of to raise money.

I got the idea on a 4th of July weekend to have a lunch stand at the end of our lane and also sell homemade ice cream. I remember thinking, "If I can just make $40 profit to buy groceries, I will be happy." When we made much more than that, I got excited about a bakery. The three oldest children could help a lot now, and one year I sold $18,000 worth. I also made and sold handmade quilts when I could.

One year when Miriam was a baby, we raised six acres of organic potatoes. We owned an old fashioned potato planter and a digger. We had a busload of my relatives from Butler County come one day to pick up the potatoes. That project didn't prove to be as profitable as the bakery.

Photos

The Amish do not allow picture taking. Most of these were taken after we knew the ban was inevitable.

This picture is of the women in my family.
I am on the far left.

One of our Amish buggies.

The buggies we used. The buggies without the "top" are the ones used for "courtship".

This is our farm in Clinton, Michigan, where we lived for 11 years. Notice the oat shocks on the hill.

This is the "Phone Shack" that some of the communities are allowed to use.

This is our home in Butler County, Indiana, where I grew up.

My 10 grandchildren at the time we left the Amish.

The school house in Austin, Michigan, where my children studied.

This is our farm in Austin, Michigan. In this photo is "Mac", our horse. We bought him for $600 out of my earnings from the bakery business.

My daughters and grandchildren. I am standing on the left with Betty to my right. Front row, left to right, are Miriam, Lorene and Marilyn.

Another photo of my daughters and their children. My daughter-in-law, Esther, is standing behind them.

Fun times with a friend in Colorado. The Colorado friend who took this photo sent it to us years later.

A funeral gathering.

This photo was taken of my three oldest children and playmates in 1980. In the background was our chicken house and barn in Clinton, Michigan. This photo was sent to us in recent years.

This is a photo of my son David when he was 17 years old. He was starting the "rebellious" years. David posed because that's what "rebellious" kids do. The forbidden camera he is holding belonged to him.

Norman and Marilyn ready for church. Norman had come to visit Marilyn before they were married. David took this photo against Marilyn's wishes.

I am with some of my grandchildren. These two photos were taken in 2010.

CHAPTER THIRTEEN

Battered Wife
More Clinton Stories

The first physical abuse incident occurred when we were in Indiana the week before my sister, Dora, got married.

We were visiting Aaron's mom one day along with about four families of his relatives. We had planned to go down to my mother's house to spend the night, but had told my half-sister, Ella, that we might stop in for supper at her place, which was right on the way. Ella had gone to Fairmont with horse and buggy and stopped by on her way home to find out for sure if we were still planning to come or not.

Aaron and the men of his family were standing outside in a circle laughing and joking. I tried to get his attention so I could give Ella an answer, but he just gave me angry looks and motioned me away. So, I told Ella, "I can't get an answer." She replied, "I really have to go, because the milking isn't done at home yet and it is high time to milk those cows."

We didn't have phones, and she desperately needed to know if she had to make supper for us. So I went out and tried again. I called louder and told him what Ella wanted to know. He cut his eyes at me, which warned me to go away. Later, he took me aside and angrily said, "I'm so mad at you for interrupting me when I'm with my relatives." But I did get my answer: "Tell her NO."

The long, 10-mile drive to my mother's house seemed extra-long because I could sense Aaron's anger. I had four-month-old baby Ivan on my lap, and we were about half way there when his anger erupted. He told me what a dumb thing I had done and how little those men thought of me, and on and on.

I was trying my best to explain the situation, when suddenly he jabbed his elbow fast and hard into my chest. Not once, not twice, but on and on until he had spent his anger. I was crying out loud but he kept right on. My arm felt like it was just hanging with no support. I was miserable with pain for years from the damage he did to one of my ribs.

From then on, milking cows was even more difficult. Thankfully, when we moved to Austin I went with a group of Amish to a chiropractor in Danville. He had to use a lot of force to fix my rib. Again, my family had no clue anything was wrong.

I helped with the field work and haymaking when I could, even sometimes when it was difficult for me. When the children got older, I cultivated corn at least a few days per season which I loved to do. Often, the children played in the lane and waited for me to make my round. I had to let the horses rest at each end.

I was on a two row cultivator pulled by two slow horses. There was a foot pedal on each side of the cultivator. When I pressed on the right pedal, the shovels moved to the left, and vice versa

I had to use my feet on those pedals to guide the little shovels. If the horses decided to step out of line, I really had to press hard on those pedals, and oh, horrors, quite a bit of corn could disappear before the horses and the shovels were straightened out. At the end of each row, I had to pull down on a big lever that lifted the shovels out of the ground. That was hard to do and it required all the strength I had.

While I was working in the fields, I would get a really dark tan on my face and arms. I remember something I did that has remained a secret until now.

Whenever I'd rest the horses at the far end of the field by the woods where not a soul could see me, I decided to see if my legs would tan, too. Somehow, it gave me a tiny feeling of independence and nobody ever found out!

Haymaking

I have mostly good memories of haying during my growing up years. It took a lot of people to put up loose hay and our large family provided plenty of help. At an early age we could drive the horses hitched to the hay wagon with the loader attached behind it. We would climb up on the "standard" that was on the front end of the wagon to help hold the hay. We had to lean forward with our legs against the standard to brace ourselves and hang on tightly to the reins that reached way up there. We were up so high we could look down on the horses' backs! That was scary!

After the hay started piling up behind us, it didn't seem so scary anymore and when it was all loaded, the hay was above our heads. Usually, two men would be on the wagon to evenly spread the hay as it came off the loader. When we were ready to go back to the barn one of them took the reins. Sometimes I stayed squashed down in the hay or they would pull me up to the top. What a thrilling ride back, especially when they let the horses trot!

After we were parked by the barn someone had to be on top of the load to stick the giant hay fork into the hay. It could get complicated when the four prongs got tangled up in the ropes. If not done properly, the load could come loose on the way up, showering the man below with hay. If the fork wasn't stuck in deeply enough, just a small load of hay would go up.

A long heavy rope was attached to the hay fork and looped through a pulley at the peak of the barn roof. The other end hooked onto the back of a cart.

Somebody drove the horses to pull the cart and the fork full of hay went up into the haymow, also called the hayloft. When it was at the right spot inside the hayloft, the man up there would holler and the horses were stopped. Then someone standing on the ground would pull a trip rope attached to the fork which released the hay. The driver of the cart would unhook the rope, and then drive it back to prepare for the next fork full, while someone else pulled back the heavy rope to hook it on again.

I think every man hated to be in the haymow. It was hard work spreading out the pile of hay with a pitchfork in the heat and dust. We always had to wait to send up the next fork full until he hollered "ready." I would guess the average load might have six forkfuls.

This might sound interesting, but let me tell you another story.

It was the summer of 1985, when David was three months old. I had not recovered yet from his birth, partly due to it being springtime with all the hard work of gardening to do, etc., plus the bursting udders of the now 25 cows we milked.

In a few weeks it would be our turn to have church at our house. Just when I needed to start cleaning and getting the house ready, the haying season began.

Talk about another impossible situation! Getting the house ready was quite a chore. Everything had to be cleaned from inside out, starting with the closets and drawers. The furniture would be stored in the bedroom or sometimes in an outside building to make room for the benches; enough to accommodate about twenty families. The host family also provided most of the food.

At this time, Betty was 12 and Alfred was 10. They were the only help we had to do the haying besides Aaron and me. The children drove in the field, while

Aaron loaded the hay by himself. Then while he was up in the haymow, Betty drove the cart. She also had to drag the heavy rope back. I wasn't able to stick the fork into the hay on the wagon, but I could tug on the trip rope and try to make sure everything went smoothly with the children's jobs. I brought a hickory rocker out by the wagon so I could rest or nurse the baby between forkfuls.

Lorene kept an eye on the baby to see if he was crying and sometimes I brought him out to nurse. Afterward she'd hold him. If things didn't always go right, we sure heard it from the haymow! Alfred tried so hard. Aaron would bark out orders from the haymow without being able to see the situation outside. Occasionally, only a small forkful went up and other times we watched the fork go up and the last bit of hay fall off before it entered the barn.

That would give me a sinking feeling, knowing what we'd hear from the haymow. Sometimes, Betty didn't hear the holler to stop. The forkful went way past the spot where it was supposed to be which didn't make for a happy trooper up there who was already hot and miserable!

Between loads I would go in and start cleaning closets for church, then the baby would fuss, and here would come another load of hay…

Now it was 10:30—time to make dinner. We ate at 11:30 and there were no sandwiches or skimpy meals! Then at 5:30, with not much cleaning done and ready to drop, those high-producing cows had to be milked, then I still had to make supper. You see, getting ready for church was all mapped out so you would be ready on time. I didn't dare fall behind because I had no family there to help me.

CHAPTER FOURTEEN

Neighbor's Kindness

While living in Clinton, about the time Betty was 13 and baby, David, was about a year old, we were all down with a bad case of the flu. It was winter time and everyone was flat on their backs, except Betty, Lorene, and me.

So the three of us milked all of those cows by ourselves, until we got sick, too. I don't remember if we hired someone or if a few of the others had gotten well enough to do the milking. Besides having the flu I developed a severe sinus infection and later had to see a doctor.

Well, one afternoon as we were lying there in our misery, our neighbor, Dan A., walked in. What he did just voluntarily out of the kindness of his heart, just blew me away. It really made up for the manure he had left on our farm years earlier.

He must have believed that onions can cure anything because he had brought a whole bunch with him! He got busy slicing and frying some of them and gave us all onion sandwiches to eat. He also made toast for each of us. Then he hung whole onions from the ceilings, which would draw in the germs from the air. You could get sick if you ever ate one of those onions! Next, he tied onion slices on the bottom of the children's feet, which helped to draw out toxins from the body. Thanks, Dan A.

One day, that first summer while we were still on probation in the community and the ministers were still coming regularly to check on us, they said a building of ours across the lane had a gray roof on it. The rules only allowed black or green for a roof. Aaron told them the building was built by the former owner who had put the roof on. It was hard to imagine that anyone had even noticed because it was a tall two-story building used to store wood and other things. And why wasn't it noticed long before? I suppose someone needed more brownie points! Shortly after that visit, Dan A. drove in and unloaded several pails of black tar, so we could cover up the gray. He didn't seem any too happy about it.

Then there's the incident when Ivan broke his leg when he was four years old. He had been running behind the plow and Aaron didn't realize that Ivan had jumped on the back and held onto the seat. Ivan's foot slipped off and went between the spokes of the wheel and as the wheel kept turning it twisted his leg until the bone broke all the way through. Fortunately, it was a clean break.

Talk about a child in pain. He shivered and shook, and those screams were so hard to bear! My girls remember how I was near panic until Aaron returned. He had gone to the neighbors to use the phone to call a driver. Sometimes it was hard to find one who wasn't busy. I was so glad to get to the emergency room where Ivan could be given some pain killers. That really relieved his pain and calmed him down.

There were some miserable days ahead when his leg got itchy under the cast. It really helped when the community put a "sunshine box" together for him. He could look forward to opening one wrapped package a day. Inside could be toys, keepsakes, or books. He even got a shirt that was handmade, which was really appreciated.

CHAPTER FIFTEEN

Clinton and Youth

I discussed with an ex-Amish friend what went through her mind in the rebellious years during her youth. I asked if her feelings about eternity had been like our son David's had been and many others. She said, "No, not exactly." She had held onto a tiny thread of hope that being Amish would somehow get her to heaven.

She would compare herself to the "English" people and think, "What about them?" believing her chances were better than theirs. Deep down though, she felt bad, really bad. She tried to describe how awfully she had suffered even though, on the surface, it looked like she was having a good time.

She was often tormented with so much fear of not going to heaven that she actually broke down when trying to describe it. She said, "Wow, there's some more healing needed in my heart!" She is thankful to be out of that bondage so she can be healed.

It is just so sad that Amish people aren't taught how to receive salvation and are not allowed to listen to or read anything other than their own teachings. On the day we attended Amish church for the last time, the preacher spoke to the four or five youth that had started instructions for baptism. He spoke directly to them and said, "You beloved young souls, all that is required of you to prepare for baptism is to be obedient to your parents and the church."

He repeated it to make it very clear how simple it was. My heart aches for those young people and I pray that God will open that closed door so they might receive Jesus and experience the peace and joy of salvation. Who wouldn't want to trade peace for feelings of guilt and fear or rebellion?

I am going to explain about the Amish *deaning* (in German), meaning fellowship with other like communities. When a community becomes too liberal, conservative communities don't *dean* or fellowship with them any longer. After this happens, they aren't allowed to preach when they come to visit. Then there is another step. When a community allows a liberal preacher to preach, then that community gets cut off from fellowship, as well. This shunning isn't as severe as the ban would be. They can't share communion, give the holy kiss, and other minor things. Basically, they just don't go back and forth very much.

As Clinton grew bigger, it grew in power, too. When all those new communities started they had to be careful to stay close to the guidelines and rules or they would be cut off. Then they couldn't have fellowship or *dean* with anyone who fellowshipped with Clinton.

Some didn't care and just went with more liberal churches but most of them wanted to stay in that fellowship, even though it often upset them that they couldn't have some more liberal rules in their new communities. That's what has controlled most of those Midwest communities. This has caused much turmoil, conflict, and confusion.

When we first moved to Clinton, it was so hard to adjust to the fact that the ministers came to our door quite often. Until that time, it had rarely happened, maybe only one other time in my life. I had never feared the ministers or the church like this before.

I can't relate everything that went on or happened, but one thing does stand out. The ministers told us that our children needed to be disciplined more. Betty was four years old, Alfred was two years old, and Lorene was just a baby. A lot could be said about this, but what I want to say is how I felt when taking my children to church, or anywhere. I was already being scrutinized and watched regarding my clothes and I was having an awful time keeping my hair pinned up. In most communities, the hair was put up in a bun or what we called a "hairball". Here, the rules were different. We had to take the hair to the top of the head and pin it on a hair comb. Since my hair was short and thin, it was almost impossible to do and I had to re-do it several times a day. Many women developed bald spots if they had a lot of hair.

On top of all this, now I was terrified that my children wouldn't behave according to the standards. We confided some things to a young couple who moved in from Butler County. They later thanked us and said they didn't see how they would've made it through, if they hadn't known that others were treated that way, too.

Then there was the couple from Ohio with nine children who moved in. He confided in us what had happened when six months of "probation" was up, when they thought they would be taken in the church as members.

Instead, they were told they wouldn't be accepted until their children behaved better in church. That poor mother had at least five children sitting with her, plus a baby on her lap. I clearly remember sitting behind her when it was about time for them to be accepted into the church.

Her little ones were turning around and fidgeting some, and I noticed one of the super self-righteous women watching them with a look of disapproval and disgust. Most of the other children did sit very still and barely moved for those three and a half hours on a hard, backless bench.

At one time I had a secret code with my children. I didn't even want to let others see me having to straighten them out. So, I would try not to draw attention as I reached over and gave them a pinch. I tried not to turn my head much as I gave them "the look". That usually worked.

This is something that happened when Lorene was in the lower grades. They had a teacher who had married and was about four months pregnant. Apparently my smart little girl had figured out some things. So, she innocently told a classmate she thought the teacher was going to have a baby. That caused an uproar among the parents, and I was blamed for informing little Lorene about this forbidden subject!

I had no clue that she knew anything about such matters, but before I had a chance to explain, I got several really nasty letters. They were full of scolding and lectures, as though I had committed a great crime. I was also told that I had been the subject of their pious gossip at a quilting. Had they known what was happening among their own boys, who appeared as pious as their dads, they would have had something to talk about.

I guess that community was so focused on keeping everything under control that sometimes they lost sight of common sense, reasoning, and mercy.

CHAPTER SIXTEEN

Change: Another Story

While we lived in Butler County, we put up a new hog house to raise hogs.

We hired a girl to cook and care for the children for two weeks while I helped build it. A hired girl was cheaper than a hired man. I really did enjoy those two weeks. It was a pleasant change.

When the sows started farrowing (birthing), I loved to run out to the hog house when I could to watch and learn. If it was at night, we sat out there with a lantern to make sure every little piggy was saved. Aaron called them his little $20 bills. It wasn't long before he got this bright idea… you know he had a lot of work to do and needed his sleep… so he said I could just watch the piglets by myself. I saved him many a $20 bill!

According to our religion, we couldn't use any birth control, so in 1982, I was pregnant with my sixth child. This happened while we lived in Clinton, Michigan. Under pressure, I finally gave in to having my baby at home. After three days of complications, I finally started labor on a Sunday evening at chore time. I still had to milk the cows during this time. My water broke three days earlier, and I had three days of mild contractions, before the actual hard labor began. By then, I was worn out.

Aaron took the children to our neighbors and called the doctor. He did birthing the "natural" way, without any interference. He used herbs instead of medication. I preferred having a natural birth, myself, but sometimes some intervention would have helped.

Aaron started going on and on about all he needed to do the next day, and why does this have to be at night, when he needs his sleep. I saw visions of him sitting up with the sows at night when they had their babies. I truly felt I was more worthless than a dirty old pig! The doctor fell asleep on the couch and Aaron slept in a bed all night. I tried hard to be as quiet as possible so they could sleep, as I labored alone all night.

When they woke up, the doctor was afraid that something wasn't right, and was going to take me to the hospital, then changed his mind and said the baby should arrive in a few hours. He decided he was going to go make his rounds and would be back by then. Aaron did the chores and I was left alone, again.

Was I terrified? For sure! Aaron and the doctor came back in time for Marilyn to be born at 9:00 a.m.

While living in Maxville, we raised and fed pigs on contract. I really liked to help and I now had grown children, so it was much easier.

Aaron got a job as the foreman of a construction crew of six to eight Amish men. They built homes in subdivisions. Because I could now give the pigs their shots, too, Aaron could go on working.

There is one subdivision in Yuba, Nebraska where they built all of the 150 houses. They had a good driver with a pickup truck to take them to work. They couldn't own the trailer and tools so a driver or "Englisher" would buy them. I don't know how, but in some underhanded way, the tools were not owned by the Amish men.

In many ways my life was much easier in Maxville, and one of those ways was that for the first time in our lives, Aaron had a job away from home. Yeah, I will take care of the pigs!

CHAPTER SEVENTEEN

Fearful Times at Church

I want to talk about some more reasons that caused me to be fearful at times. When church services started at 9:00 in the morning, the preachers would get up from where they sat on a separate bench that faced the men. Men and women didn't sit together. In single file, with the bishop first and the deacon last, they went upstairs just as the rest of us started singing the first song.

Their main purpose was to decide whose turn it was to preach or to discuss and come to an agreement about church rules. The deacon would relate what the peoples' responses had been when he went on one of his assigned duties, "investigation calls." He was also given more assignments if they were needed. If someone had come to confess and one of the four punishments hadn't been selected, during this time the ministers would decide which one fit the misdeed or offense.

Punishments are divided into four different categories. The first one is for the tiny sins and the last one, which is the ban, is for the very worst sins. Sometimes punishment would be selected according to how well the person was liked or disliked. Anyway, they then ended their meeting with a prayer out of a prayer book and came downstairs for the sermon. If they were back down by 10:00, I'd breathe a sigh of relief.

Often it was 10:30 and if there had been bad arguing or disagreements it could be almost 11:00. At times when the ministers had my family in their sights, it could be so intimidating and fearful to see them coming down stairs looking very stern and dead serious. What made it so fearful to confess in church was how we had to go out of the room, while the ministers went around asking each member if they agreed to let us confess that day. The bishop had already broadcast the offence. If someone had seen us break a rule we had to agree to include that in our confession. If it was something we had to change, for example; too short a dress, too wide a belt, or a cap too "*stolz*" we could not confess that day. A man's hair might be too short, his beard shaved down too far, or it could involve buildings or machinery. Whatever they were, the changes would have to be made before we were allowed to try again in two weeks. It was a great relief when we were called back in, sat on the bench facing the ministers, and the bishop said, "We have a unanimous 'yes' vote and you can confess!"

It was also a common sight to see the ministers in a group before church out by the shed or somewhere. Sometimes they needed more time than they had with an hour upstairs to discuss a situation and come to an agreement. A fearful sight it was, too, when we didn't know who or what they were discussing. You could never tell; it might be about you.

They could also have a lot of ill feelings toward each other and sometimes a minister or a bishop would become a victim and get picked on just like the rest of us. There was always someone in the community who knew exactly what to do to earn brownie points from the bishop.

That person would go to the bishop in a sober and serious way and act like he was very concerned and wanted to help build up the church. He would report things about the other members.

Often, it was just a honey-coated way to get even with someone. My dad saw through people like that, but some bishops fell for it and gave the guy a pat on the back. It sure was best to stay on the good side of someone like that. Anyway, I would think, "How can this be right, to be in a church where you have so much fear, even when you are trying to obey the rules?"

When we first moved to Clinton, Michigan, I caused a new rule to be added to the *ordnungs letter,* or rule book. "*Ordnungs* church" was the day the rules were read during the meeting. I know the new rule was still being "read" years after we moved away and it might still be read twice a year during their *ordnungs* church.

This is how it came about. One day in church, I was sitting beside my neighbor Ida Schmucker. Bishop Abe Stutzman's wife sat behind us and I noticed she was wiping tears all morning. After church she took me aside and asked me if my apron belt was wider than 1 ½ inch, if I was sure it wasn't any wider than that? I said, "I never make it wider, that I know of." She told me to go home and measure it and if it wasn't more than 1 ½ inch, to just ignore what she said. Well, it was a 16th inch less than 1 ½ inch all around, except for a small area in the back which was exactly what the rules said.

So 2 weeks later, I told her what the measurements were and this is what they added in that *ordnungs* letter, where it says what the width of the belt should be. Now, they admonish and tell the church not to make the apron belts so close to 1 ½ inch because you almost can't tell if it is wider or not. So, that would be like a rule upon a rule, wouldn't it?

What was so bizarre is that the woman beside me had a belt that was a tad wider than mine! She didn't come from Butler County, I guess.

Clinton Stories

I want to talk about what happens when a woman tries to get help if she has an abusive husband. Let's just say there is no recourse for battered women in the Amish community.

I knew of a woman whose first husband had died and she married again. I had sensed that there was something very wrong in her life, and later it was proven that I was right. I would like to go into a lot more detail about her situation, but I want to protect her identity. I sure don't want her to have any more encounters with the bishops and the church.

I heard that she had been talking here and there, and even went to the ministers for help. Well, all they did was to tell her she needed to stop talking to anyone about her husband. She and I didn't know each other very well and probably never had a real conversation until the day Aaron and I stopped in. A driver took us to her house because Aaron had some farm business he needed to do with her husband.

I knew it would take some time, so I decided to go in and visit with her. She met me at the door and stepped outside with me for more privacy to talk. I listened as she poured out her heart as fast as she could. My heart broke for her. I wanted to just hold her and pray for her, but Amish people don't do that. I was so astonished that she trusted me, since she didn't know about my circumstances. I think that often a hurting woman intuitively knows when another woman is hurting, and she felt I would understand. I just want to say that religious spirits and compassion do not mix.

From experience, I've observed that the more rules, the more cold hearts and immorality. The Bible tells about similar men that Jesus had to deal with. Be thankful if you only read about them and don't have to go through the experience. Again, I'm not talking about all Amish people, or all communities.

It was hard to understand the way I was being treated by the most "righteous" community that I knew of while living in Clinton. I gave birth to 4 of my children there. I was very sick and weak during the time I was pregnant with Ivan.

After his birth, I was depressed and I suffered my first breakdown. By the grace of God, I don't have any hatred against the Clinton Amish community, but I pray they get their focus on Jesus, instead of on the rules and each other.

I would often wish for some calamity to happen, like an earthquake or something, and figured that might help change their focus. At least when they would be digging me out, they wouldn't be checking the width of my belt, or would they?

CHAPTER EIGHTEEN

Move to Austin, Michigan

We lost the farm and moved to Austin, Michigan, in 1988. (I cried my way through writing about this experience!)

We were not alone. Many farmers lost their property during those years because the interest rate had shot up to 18 percent.

My husband's brother wound up buying the farm, and we farmed 50/50, dividing the income. We did this for four years before we realized it was a no-win situation.

I guess losing the farm was a blessing in disguise because it was like a tool to help get us out of Clinton. It had helped a lot that my brother Atlee moved to Clinton about two years before, to get his children away from Butler County, but they only stuck it out for 11 months. He decided that he wasn't going to take the stuff we did, and by then other communities had been started, so they moved to Austin, Michigan. I had been really heartbroken when they moved. I was so glad when we were together again.

When you have a relative in the community, people don't gossip as much about you. Also, your relatives can speak up and set things straight. I had always felt like a chicken without feathers, unprotected.

We got a farm that an Amish man had lost. The bank sold it to us for a very low price. It was about four miles away from the main community. I really enjoyed the freedom I had that summer!

We had lived in the midst of the community in Clinton, with a schoolhouse on our land. I was always in fear; afraid the kids would hear or see something and report it. When we moved, after losing the farm, that outrageous financial burden was lifted that had been hanging over us for 4 years. It was nice not to be criticized for little things like buying a ball and bat for our 10 year old son. It was a reward for doing a good job of cultivating a big field of corn.

We now had a Woodmizer sawmill which gave us extra income, so we only needed to milk half as many cows. It was here I milked my last cow. After the cow kicked me into the gutter, my children said it wasn't necessary that I help anymore.

We had a swing in a big tree in the yard and I often used it. Oh, the bliss as I reached for the skies and sang songs of praise, in German.

In Austin, life was easier. Betty was 15 years old then and out of school. Alfred still had two months left to finish 8th grade.

Here, the environment was a lot different. This community was a lot more "carnal" and outspoken and the gossip wasn't pious. The attitude toward us was much better, and the ministers were less intimidating. My brother Atlee was ordained a minister soon after we moved. The ministers always gathered in the ordained family's home after church for supper.

I was there helping with supper when the first people arrived. Minister Raymond Lambright started joking and laughing with my sister-in-law Katie and me. I thought, "Wow, he's human like us!"

In 1989, my sister Malinda, her husband, Albert Kauffman, and family moved to Austin. It sure was a good feeling to have more of my family closer again.

Then, in 1990, Aaron told me we needed to start a bakery, because it was tough getting on our feet financially. I said, "I simply can't do it." I was still recovering from the hard work in Clinton, but I had no choice, so I did it. Sister Malinda helped by making noodles and candies. The inspector was stricter and we couldn't have customers coming to the house. A Mennonite man who had a bulk food store would pick up the baked goods and sell them in his store.

Also, the inspector required us to have a hot water heater. The church had already allowed them in the milk house, just homemade, welded together from tin or stainless steel, and heated with a kerosene heater underneath. There was a big fuss and disagreement about whether it should be allowed in the bakery. I guess common sense won that time and we got it, but we weren't supposed to take any of that hot water to the main part of the house to use.

By August, I was so very tired from overwork and stress that I wound up in the hospital for four days. This was not the first such episode. I had experienced similar heart attack-like symptoms several times before, on the farm in Clinton. Later, the doctors would diagnose my condition as pericarditis, an inflammation in the heart lining. After I recovered, the children and I started making baskets to sell. An older lady taught me how to do it. We had to dye the reeds, and then weave them. This work was much easier than baking and I enjoyed it.

The community had just three districts. Eli Hochstetler was our bishop, and the other two were Aaron Schrock and Joe Yutzy. Wow! They sure had free speech here and plenty of fighting! After some of the comments I heard, I'd think, "Hey, you better go hide under your bed till the coast is clear." I expected the deacon would be sent to admonish, but nothing ever happened. The ministers didn't admonish the church against gossip. It seemed they enjoyed it too much themselves. At one time, the women had regular quilting bees to raise money for the schools. The gossip got so bad I would come home and fall across the bed, feeling disgustingly sick down to my toes. You see, when you hear all that about others, you can be certain you'll eventually be on their list, too.

Another family tragedy happened in 1990, when I wasn't quite well yet from the heart episode I had several months earlier. My brother, Joseph, was killed at age 33. His youngest child was almost due, and was born three weeks after the funeral. He and my brother Marvin, and their wives, lived on the home farm, in separate houses, since they both had married. They all had just moved to a new community in Reedsburg, Illinois, only six weeks before. He was working on the roof of a building close to the road. A piece of tin that he was holding hit the electric wires and he was electrocuted. Marvin tried C.P.R. until help came, but it was instant death. It took about two years before Marvin started to be himself again, his grief was so devastating.

Austin was fairly good for us until the last year and a half before we moved, although it was hard to see others being treated so pathetically! Usually the gossipers would pick on someone until they couldn't take it anymore and moved out, and then you'd wonder, "Who's next?"

Eventually, after our friends Harvey Nisley, his family, and my brother Atlee and his family, moved out, it was our turn. It is so sad when bishops and ministers use their position and power to act on their personal grudges and hatred. It started when Lorene turned 17 and we let her date Aden Mast, a boy that the community didn't think was good enough for her. His mom and family moved in from a liberal community in Kansas. His dad had left the family years ago.

It seemed some other boys had figured on dating Lorene. Aden had sincerely joined the church and got baptized. Yes, he had the same big, bushy and black hair that he had later. There had been no complaints and the bishops were o.k. at the time he was baptized. But later, when the hatred started, it became absolutely impossible for Aden to please them with that hair. He actually hated his hair. It was naturally bushy, but he was accused of styling it that way. They judged him as being *"stolz"* or proud.

Then we couldn't do anything right either. I suppose if we would've "tin-canned" the boy and send him down the road, we would've been fine. I am glad we didn't. Today he's a good husband and father, and wonderful son-in-law.

After Aden had moved to Austin, he worked for a couple who needed help on their farm. When all the uproar was going on about him dating our daughter, the wife talked to me about Aden and encouraged me not to pay attention to the talk. She said he was a very good worker, kind and considerate, and did things around the house without being asked, etc.

Another rule was, the men couldn't have any hair showing on their foreheads between the hat and the eyebrows. It was hard to keep it under the hat and often they weren't aware that some hair was showing. That sure created lots of "road work" for the poor deacons! By now the deacon was a common sight at our house. You could recognize that familiar horse from quite a distance. I'd run to my bedroom, get on my knees and pray until I was told to come outside, too. What now? Often we didn't have any clue what the problem might be. We had been fine for the first five years.

Aden, his mom and siblings, moved to Maxville when we did. He was accepted there. Austin was off the chart the way they would pick on people and gossip about them.

My son, Alfred, had found a girlfriend, Esther Troyer, in Belmont, Wisconsin. He met her at a wedding there. They got married in 1995, just before we moved again.

Before moving, we had a farm sale like we did seven years before in Clinton. This time I had help to prepare food for the lunch stand and bake sale. It seemed strange to get voluntary help. I had my small children to help me prepare for the bake sale and lunch stand in Clinton, but it was still way too much for me. My heart had acted up again and I just collapsed that night. I truly didn't think I'd be alive the next morning. I didn't much care either. I had also fallen down the outside cellar steps and had another miscarriage before we moved to Austin.

CHAPTER NINETEEN

My Mother's Death

My parents had moved a house against the main house and connected them, which is the way most people did when they got older. Brother Joseph and Ada Kauffman had already been announced to the church to be married, when dad died in the middle of the wedding preparations. He died from a heart attack in 1977. We stayed for their wedding which took place a week after the funeral.

Joseph and Ada moved into the house across the road. Sister Malinda married Albert Kauffman later that year. Dora married Albert's brother Lester in 1979. There were many changes.

Before long, brother Marvin had built a house, barn, shed, and hog house a little way up the road from Joseph's, and Lester and Dora moved into the big house. Then in 1990, Joseph and Marvin moved to Reedsburg, Illinois. Lester and Dora also moved there in 1992, the year our mother died. They built a big new house and attached a cute little house for mother. But, with my brother's death, and all the changes, it was just too much for mother with her failing health.

Lester and Dora brought mother to us for awhile until their house was finished and they were moved in. Mother went from bad to worse fast. She did not want to be waited on and fought hard to do things for herself. She only lived in her new house for six weeks before she died.

I was there 24/7 during that time, because it was too much for my sister Dora to handle and take care of all her little children. Mother needed constant care. A feeding tube had been inserted through a hole in her stomach, plus she was on oxygen and medications. She suffered so much pain and had difficulty breathing, because of fluid on her lungs. She would often beg for air. Her weight was down to 60 pounds near the end.

We, the surviving six children, were all around her bedside when she died. It was breathtaking to see her when she was brought back from the undertaker! Glorious peace was on her face and no pain! We cried and laughed with relief and joy, and mourned later.

Living the 19th Century in the 20th Century
The Outhouse Story

Each family has only one outhouse and the females mostly use it. Males never use them at gatherings, but occasionally they will use the outhouse at home. Otherwise, their jobs are done in corners of the barn.

The average outhouse had two big holes and a smaller one for children. Some had three big holes, and I've seen some with four.

On church days, or during other events, there could be several people waiting in line. Instead of going in one person at a time, quite a few would go in. They would wait their turns until all were finished, then out they came and more people went in. This crowding happened mostly when the weather was windy or cold.

Many times the edges weren't smooth, which made it uncomfortable. I hated to sit on the middle hole. When I wanted to get up, there was no privacy. If I waited for the others to get up first, they didn't have any privacy! I liked the two holers better!

In the earlier years, we used Sears and Montgomery Wards catalogues for our toilet paper. Here's a tip: Choose the plain pages with no colored pictures. They're not so stiff and don't scratch as badly!

Ever so often, the outhouse had to be cleaned. This is how it was done. A man who was given that responsibility had to take a few boards off of the backside and forked the piles out into a wheelbarrow. Since it was such a hateful job, sometimes it would get very full before the man got around to it. Had enough?

Other Inconveniences

We never had indoor bathrooms, just outhouses. It's kind of miserable in the cold winter, especially if the door had blown open and the seat was covered with snow! We had granite chamber pots in the house to use if we had to get up during the night. That could be a pleasant chore the next day!

We took a bath with a round galvanized pail called a foot tub. In the winter we'd block off an area behind the stove with curtains for privacy.

In the summer we'd bathe in our rooms upstairs. Saturday was normally bath day. Sometimes baths were taken on other days, too, when we went to doctor's appointments or other events.

Head washing and haircuts were done every other week. The girls' hair was braided every week, until they were out of school. Then their hair was put up like the adults, in a bun, or "hairball".

The men's hair had to be combed straight down and cut a certain length around the head. It couldn't be shorter than the middle of the ears. Usually, it was haircut time every two weeks.

We got a bigger galvanized water tub where we could at least sit in a few inches of water. It was a big chore to heat all that water and hard to dump it into a pail to throw out. It was in 1991 that we had to stop at a motel and for first time in my life I had a shower. Wow! I didn't sleep well that night, so I got up several times and took a few more showers! I would think of the wonderful luxury and advantage the president had. Yeah, he had a lot of stress, but he could get totally relaxed under that shower!

There are some things about the oil stove that I didn't like. Often, the burners didn't burn right or smoked. If the wick needed to be changed, it was nearly impossible. It sure took the joy out of cooking. This kind of stove has caused many fires or smoke damage.

Sometimes, I would leave something on a burner to cook, or bake, while I went out to do the milking. I would make sure the burner was turned down low, but sometimes when I came in to check it, the flames were out of control. That caused black soot to settle on everything! If it was bad enough, even the walls and ceilings had to be washed. I didn't like the wood cook stove either. Often, I didn't have the right size or kind of wood, or it was too green, or too dry. I sure appreciate my electric stove.

When we moved to Maxville, we bought a house from an "Englisher". It had electricity and bathrooms, hot water, and modern conveniences. We were given more time than other communities would have allowed; about three months to change, or rather, tear up everything.

Here, we were allowed bathrooms, but no toilet stools. We still had to heat the water for the tub, but at least it had a drain. The other luxuries I enjoy now are my vehicle, stove, fridge, washer, dryer, phone, electricity, and especially lights that snap on. It wasn't easy to come home at night with small children and stumble in the dark till you got a kerosene lamp lit.

A wall had to be torn out so we could set up the kitchen wood stove. We took out the three toilet stools, and moved an outhouse that we bought from an old couple. Then we had to disconnect the electricity and tear out the carpet. Basically, we had to make sure everything met the requirements for the rules in this community.

We had to build an insulated building to hold a 2,000-gallon tank that would hold the water which was pumped in. The tank had to be a certain height so the water could go into the house and other buildings by gravity flow. The water from the faucets now flowed a lot slower since there was no more pressure. Since we no longer had electricity, we had to use a gas motor on the pump. When the tank got empty and water stopped coming from the faucets, the motor needed to be filled with gas and started. The water wasn't very cold in the summertime.

After all this was done, supposedly we were now separate from the world.

Do you think that transition was easy after three months of bliss? The rules for dress were more liberal, just small things to change. For once, I didn't have to rip up clothes and re-do them, like the width of shirt collars, belts, seams on the bottom of aprons and dresses, etc.

A big problem we were having was finding a dependable "taxi driver". This is a person who was paid to take us places since we didn't own cars ourselves. We had to bother our neighbors to use their phone (before getting the phone shack) and often when we needed to go somewhere we couldn't find a driver. Finally, we found some low-lifes in Pittsfield who were often late or didn't show at all. We didn't have a phone to call and ask when or if they were coming. To put it mildly, it was frustrating! We missed my nephew's wedding in Indiana because of a no-show.

Another thing I think is sad is how some people tried, and did, take advantage of the drivers by getting them to charge less. I felt sorry for the drivers because some of them were poor and didn't have jobs. To save money some of the men liked to hire the low-lifes. It's crazy how these men sent their wives and children to town, or on the road, with them. I shudder to think of some I drove with. I was pretty naive back then, but had I known then what I know now, I would've been scared. Anyway, I started praying for God to send us a good driver. And wow, did he answer my prayers! In the spring of 2001, Michael and Bethany Smith moved from Pennsylvania to the little town of Pittsfield. God not only answered my prayers, He doubled and tripled my expectations for a driver!

I will be forever grateful to Michael and Bethany for being our friends and encouraging us, during that difficult time. They never tried to convince us to leave the Amish community, but God just had them there to make the painful transition more bearable when we did leave. Although there are miles between us now we are still friends.

CHAPTER TWENTY

Move to Maxville

We moved to Maxville, Nebraska in 1995. We were only the eighteenth family, so there was just one district. However, it grew quickly, and it wasn't long before it was divided. This meant more ordinations would take place to make sure that all districts had the required number of ministers. Communion services were held two times a year and that's when the ordinations took place. This was a dreaded event for most, since nobody had a clue if they would be chosen. They were chosen by lots.

Here, it was more liberal in small things and, overall, I liked it better than any other community. There seemed to be a balance between the Austin and Clinton extremes. I believe many of the people had been victims of church abuse and found refuge at this community. Bishop Obed Troyer and Minister Amos

Keim and some others, had been victims of Greenville, Iowa.

I really feel for bishops whose hearts are right and have good intentions. Obed tried hard to use common sense; he'd say, "Let's be reasonable." I could tell he was a very hurt man. Sometimes a minister or two can make life miserable for a good bishop, too. No one ever wanted the position of minister, deacon or, worst of all, bishop. Someone who held one of these positions could never resign. It was for life.

Lorene married Aden Mast in 1996. The responsibility of the mother who has to be in charge of a wedding is unbelievable. My half-brother Ben's wife, Ida, from Butler County, had four girls who were married already. She was a good cook and manager, so I asked her for an outline, and recipes and amounts to prepare, etc. She sent me five sheets of instructions, which was a lifesaver! After the wedding, Aden and Lorene moved into a trailer house that we moved onto our property. After they moved to Wisconsin a few years later, we helped Betty buy the community store. We set up shelves in that trailer house for bulk food, dishes, toys and a variety of things that Amish people buy. She just loved it and became happier and more sociable.

A schoolhouse was built on our land and they had made a rule that girls couldn't teach school until they were 17. They had looked far and wide for a teacher with no success, so I was asked to do the job. I was already swamped with sewing for everybody, but as usual, I couldn't say no. But, I said, "Only if my 16 year old daughter, Miriam, may help me," and they agreed.

After awhile I'd help a little in the mornings and afternoons, and the rest of the day I would go home to sew. Miriam then taught alone the next year, and Marilyn taught two terms after that.

In 1999, Aaron wanted to try to raise organic tomatoes. We put out 700 plants, covered the ground with plastic, and irrigated, so they didn't need as much care before they started ripening. Those tomato plants really produced and we had a hard time finding enough places to sell them to. I did most of the selling. At that time, I had a driver with a closed pickup truck.

The worst part was picking the tomatoes in the late afternoon. We put them in five-gallon pails and carried them downstairs, sorted them and laid them out on tables. We got 30, five-gallon pails in one day during peak production. Aaron had said the men would help when they got home from work, but they got home later than usual.

Yep, you guessed, it was the girls and I that did it. I re-injured my back, which caused me to have excruciating pain for the next five years. Sitting in church on those hard benches was plain torture. I have received some miraculous healings since we left the Amish community. They don't believe in that at all.

Miriam married William Shetler in 2000, Ivan married Alma Yutzy in 2001, and Marilyn married Norman Yoder in 2002. In this community, I felt loved by many and my services were in high demand. When my girls were old enough to do the regular chores, I did sewing for others. I made men's suits and lots of caps, or head coverings. There were many rules for a cap, even how they had to be ironed. The rules varied in each community. It seemed the caps were used most often to determine if someone was *stolz* and if they needed admonishing or rebuking. That was another thing that kept the deacon pretty busy.

Using the treadle sewing machine was hard on my back so, finally I decided to make men's suits for my relatives only. Not many women could make the *mutza*, which male members had to wear for church services. The *mutza* is a suit coat that has a slit in the back similar to what "English" men wear. They are closed with hooks and eyes and in the front, the bottom corners have to be rounded.

People started coming from other communities asking me to make clothes for them. When I'd have to say no, they wanted me to just make a cap pattern. Few heads and amount of hair are alike, so it's often difficult to get it to fit right.

Sometimes they brought their boys so I could make patterns. A mother would bring her son and show me where his pants didn't fit right, so I would design a pattern from my boys' patterns. I taught a girl and a young mother how to make a men's m*utza* so now at least someone else could do it in that community.

Another thing I did was to get fruit and deliver it to everybody. I had to go near St. Charles, Missouri, to the peach and apple orchards. They all put their orders in, so I knew how many bushels to get. The way it started was, the people who had been getting the fruit were told they couldn't get anymore. It seemed the guy was upset about something. So I was asked if I would go try to deal with him. I had no problem. I got lots of beautiful peaches and apples in the next few years. I say all this so you can see how accepted I was and how it turned into such hate later, because someone discovered the Bible in my purse. I also couldn't hide my joy from finding the way to salvation and discovering the truth in the Bible, and that's when the rumors started.

My Testimony

I want to share my testimony in this book because there aren't many Amish people who know or understand why we left. It was in August, 2001, after I got back from delivering peaches to the community, when I started having one of those heart episodes. It had been years since I experienced the last one.

Michael and Bethany had met us a few months earlier and started driving the Amish about that time. When Michael took me to town, he thought I should see a doctor, but I refused. I told him they wouldn't find anything wrong with my heart anyway. I was experiencing heart attack symptoms and it was difficult to breathe. So, after we got home, Michael had Bethany take me to the emergency room. This time the EKG machine was saying there was something wrong.

The doctor started me on IV bags and sent me to a larger hospital. I was sure this was it, and the expression on the doctor's face told me the same thing. At this hospital, they inserted a catheter through a vein in my groin to my heart and found inflammation in the heart lining. They called my condition, pericarditis.

What was so different this time was that I had no fear of death. It was so beautiful and peaceful. I had recently gotten a new sewing machine and there was a tract with it. The title was, "Do you know you can have eternal life?"

I really wanted to read it, but you're taught not to read stuff like that because it is really deceiving. It was so tempting to read it because I had often made the remark, "I wish I knew that I could go to heaven," and I'd think, "I know why Jesus could do what he did, because he knew he was God's son, and he knew he would go to heaven."

Most of my life, I felt so much guilt and condemnation about every little thing. How can you get close to someone who you believe is always displeased with you? It's kind of hard to feel love for someone you picture as having a whip to keep you in line.

Well, I got that tract out and read it. An ex-Amish person had written it to specifically explain the plan of salvation in a way that was so perfect for someone Amish to understand.

I remember the spot where I was standing. I had just finished reading the tract and was still holding it in my hand, when the Holy Spirit touched me. Deep down in my soul, He pushed these words, "I know, that I know, that I know."

The sinner's prayer was in the tract, at the very end. After I had the experience with the Holy Spirit, I prayed that prayer!

Nothing can describe the joy I experienced when that heavy burden was lifted! The Bible opened up for me like never before. Nothing can take that away from me. Sometimes after that, when I was on a walk, I'd suddenly realize who I am in Christ. My joy would be so overwhelming; I'd leap for joy and hop and skip and say, "I am the Child of the King!"

And now, the question is, "Who deceived me?"

According to the Amish, someone must have done it, you know. The number one suspect was Michael. At first, they accused him of subverting me, and then dropped that idea because he moved away. And now, they will probably say it was that God-forbidden tract that I read.

In the end they came to the conclusion that I read the Bible too much. Some women said that they are almost afraid to read it at all because of what it did to me. All this happened to me before I ever talked to Michael about the Bible. After that, we discussed it a lot.

I never had any intentions of leaving the Amish community while all these things were happening. About 2 months before we left, I no longer cared, and somehow I knew I wouldn't go to hell if they did ban me.

I've always had a hunger for more than the stale 300 year old sermons which were all we were ever allowed to hear.

Often, after we came home from church, I would go on a walk and just cry out to God for more. I felt hungry and empty, and I would even talk to Aaron about it. I'd tell him, "We can't go on like this. I know there is more to it, to get to heaven, than this."

He would just argue that what we were doing was enough. "We are going to church every two weeks and, as long as we obey the rules and we do the best we know, we are fine."

I kind of laugh to myself now, "So, you just listen to the preaching every two weeks, and sleep through a good bit of the sermon." Aaron did see a lot of truth by the time we were banned and he left with the rest of us.

So, who was responsible for my salvation? I say it was the Holy Spirit, sent by my loving Savior, Jesus Christ, to lift me out of darkness into Light.

Thank you, Jesus.

CHAPTER TWENTY ONE

Charlotte Wedding

It would take up too much space to start at the beginning of that 1 ½ year ordeal, before we were banned, so I'll just relate some episodes. Things happened that are still too painful to think about. I could never have endured it if I wasn't doing it for Jesus. That strength could only have come from Him!

This is my son David's story as he related it to me. Many of the rebellious young people believe there's no way they can follow the rules, so they have little hope of getting to heaven. That was David's belief. He said the preaching was so much about hell and obeying the rules that he figured if he broke one little rule he'd go to hell, so he might as well break them all. During those years when he was rebellious, he hoped he wouldn't get killed; he tried to block out any thoughts about eternity. He hoped he'd get through until; somehow, he would change his mind. He couldn't find a solution, there was nothing to show him a way out, or point him to salvation.

This is the case with many Amish young people who leave home. Often they don't want to have much to do with God or any churches. I wish someone could tell them that the God they were taught to believe in, is also a loving God, and they could experience the great love He has for them. Many believe they have to go back to the Amish community to make things right, and this would be their only hope of ever getting to heaven at all. I wish there were more people who would help them get to know the real Jesus.

David had gotten a shingle haircut, which tapered in the back down to the neck. He looked just like an "English" boy, and was banned for four months, until it was all grown back again.

Some ex-Amish who knew Daniel Lapp asked him to stop by to encourage us, because they had found out we were seeing the truth. That was an enjoyable night of learning more truth, yet it was also fearful. We were afraid a buggy would drive in and we would be asked questions about who this man was. Daniel invited us to a revival in Missouri which was several months away.

David was still in this rebellious state of mind, when he saw his family being saved all around him. He resisted very hard. He went along to the revival because all the rest of us went, but he wasn't having any part of it.

For the first time ever, he heard a very different sermon! It made a difference that the preacher, Daniel Lapp, was spirit filled and Christ-like. When the invitation was given that evening, people went forward. Daniel kept pleading. Finally, David went forward and received Jesus as his personal Savior. At last he found the life line he had been groping for in the dark. I wish all Amish could find it. My joy was so great that day!

He was just 18 years old when he got saved at that revival.

We went to a wedding in Charlotte, Minnesota, where he was a table waiter with his girlfriend, Edna. It was my deceased brother Joseph's daughter, Susan, one of the twins, who got married. Imagine my prayers for David that day, seeing him with those perverted young folks who knew him as a drinking buddy, and who knows what else. I will never forget what a clean and peaceful look he had that day.

Michael's son-in-law, Pat, was our driver. We were sitting in his car waiting for David to finish eating that night, so he could go home with us. Well, most of the wedding assembly was going to make sure that wouldn't happen. It was dark that night and they used gas lamps and lanterns to light up the entire house. They pulled a buggy up beside our car and set a lantern on top so they could keep an eye on us, while many others were crouching in the dark, to make sure we wouldn't leave with David.

Finally, David came out of the house, surrounded by others to make sure we couldn't talk. He stuck his head in the car window and whispered, "Mom, you have to go home without me. I can't get away." He added, "I'm going home with Edna and her parents to Lamar, Iowa." Then he looked all around at the mob and said, "See, it's impossible."

In Lamar, the youth were really bad, and David was very popular. I was filled with terror for a while; concerned that he would be led astray again. I had no choice but to trust God. It was so amazing how God used this situation. Nobody suspected that he was saved. He was still Amish and not shunned, so secretly he accomplished a lot.

Norman Yoder and Marilyn had moved to Lamar after they were married. Edna is one of Norman's sisters. David went to visit Ivan and Alma in Wisconsin to make sure they were doing okay, after the revival, since we now couldn't have any contact with them. Then he started talking to Norman, Marilyn and Edna about salvation. Edna hadn't come to the point of being saved yet, but was totally committed to David. One night Norman saw the truth and accepted Jesus.

He was so excited; he shook David's hand and said, "Hey, we're brothers in Christ now!" Norman called Michael to drive me to the phone shack so he could tell me the good news.

"Hey Mom, I'm saved!" Norman said to me. Oh, my cup was running over with answered prayer!

Norman and Marilyn's baby, Ruthann, was only six weeks old and was Norman's parents' first grandchild.

In the meantime, Norman and David tried to talk to his mom, hoping she would see the truth. She just got hysterical, and Norman knew he couldn't handle that pressure for long. He called Michel to get Aden on the phone and said, "Get a U-Haul and come get us as soon as possible." There was a wedding in the community where everyone was that day. Marilyn wasn't able to go.

In no time, Michael had Aden, the girls and me on the road. Norman called us once, "C'mon where are you?" His parents, Noah and Anna, had come over to his house after the wedding, and he was back in the woods praying to hang on till we got there. His Mom was really beside herself, stomping and screaming. She saw Marilyn's Bible was in English and acted like it was evil, and said, "Burn it! That thing deceived you." She took the baby and said to her, "Oh my, you're going to hell." She meant that if baby Ruthann's parents took her out of the Amish, then she would wear "English" clothes and would go to hell just for that.

Norman's parents had left before we arrived. We loaded everything onto the truck. Aden drove the U-Haul back to Nebraska. The first thing Michael did was take us to the wedding to talk to David. He knew he had to get out fast now! Nobody found out what happened until the next day. I feel sorry for the parents, but we can't help if they want to stay in darkness. We wouldn't shun them, but they shun us. So who's separating who? My in-law children have heartbreaking stories of their first attempts, after being banned, to see their parents and families. One night, David called Aden to make arrangements to get him and Edna and meet up the road in an old barn, about midnight.

When Aden and Lorene arrived, there was a thunderstorm going on, and the kids didn't show up for a long time. They were having some difficulties. The ladder to the upstairs window didn't reach far enough, but David helped Edna over the edge and hung on to her until her feet touched the top rung of the ladder. They would stop at every noise and hold their breath. Then lightning would light up everything and the dog started barking. David had to get out by himself, which was nearly impossible.

Imagine how wet they were when they got to the old barn! Aden and Lorene picked them up and brought them home to Nebraska. I don't recall how long Edna had been with us, but she was in "English" clothes already and David was playing the tapes of the preaching at the revival where he got saved, and helping her understand about salvation. One day, a van drove in with her dad, Noah, some of her uncles and my two brothers from Charlotte!

My daughters and Edna had taken some laundry to Michael's brother Stan in Pittsfield, because we didn't have washers and dryers yet. David ran in a wide circle to the phone shack to call Stan's and warn them, and also to hide. He didn't especially care to see the men! It ended up the men called the cops and forced Edna to go home because she wasn't quite 18 yet. She told David to come get her in three weeks when she would be 18. Aden, Lorene, and David tried, but it was impossible.

Her dad, Noah, railed and screamed at them, and when Aden attempted to get out of the vehicle, Noah sic'd the dog on him. Lamar is the community where my sister Malinda lived. Her family knew a lot of truth, but hadn't left the Amish community yet.

During this time, Malinda's married daughter, Emma, had to use the outhouse while in church one Sunday. Edna went, too. She talked really fast and basically told how badly she was being treated. Her dad got so angry when she didn't recant her belief that he hit her. Her parents kept her in their sight every moment.

Edna was also being forced to join the church. Then David got a very confusing letter saying she was done with him and to never again try to get her. We probably won't ever know, but it sure seemed like she had been forced to write that letter. Not long before that time she had sent a letter that sounded entirely different.

David has been happily married to an "English" girl, Kathleen Owens since 2009.

When we came back from that revival, we had plans to keep it a secret as long as we could. Our son-in-law, William was so very excited about what he had heard at the revival. He was sure he could go back home and convert his buddies who worked in the carpenter crew.

Well, it didn't quite work out that way. It wasn't long before three or four of the ministers made their rounds to all of us in the evenings. There was one rumor that never died no matter how often we denied it. They insisted that we had other versions of the Bible, which they consider as false. I even showed my King James Version Bible to the bishop. He looked it over and said he couldn't find anything wrong with it.

We never had any other Bible except that we read it in English now. They tried their best to get some "sense" into us, but avoided talking about the Scriptures as much as they could. I guess the ministers were afraid of being deceived like they thought we were.

On the evening they came to Aden and Lorene, Aden took the Bible out to show them that it was only the harmless King James Version. They couldn't find fault with it, but warned them not to read so much.

When they talked to William and Miriam, she also took the Bible out and was told to take it back in before they even started talking.

They told all of us that evening to come to church and confess for going to that revival and we must stop having Bible study and not read the Bible in English. We simply could not do that. To us it would be denying Jesus and confessing to God and the church that the revival preaching was heresy.

The day they banned us, we hadn't gone to church, so the ministers came to let us know that we had been banned. They said it sounded very pitiful as the whole church cried and wailed out loud. I just wish they could have known that they weren't giving us over to the devil. Somewhere during this time my brothers and sisters came from Charlotte, Minnesota with a van driver on two different occasions.

They tried so hard to convince us we were wrong. That is hard to do when someone's understanding of the Bible is so limited. I truly felt sorry for them. I noticed that my sister, Dora, didn't say anything to argue against us. Several times she almost smiled at me, but I had no way of knowing what she was thinking. She now says, after listening to both sides, she saw that we were right.

The wedding of my niece, Susan, that we attended in Charlotte, took place the week before we were banned. I didn't want to go, but Aaron insisted. I guess people had heard that we had decided to confess, so they were nice to us. Then at about 4:00 o'clock that afternoon my brothers talked to Aaron about it. Aaron told them, "We're not planning to confess." They said, "You need to get off this place, right now!"

When I found out, I wanted to leave, but Aaron said we needed to wait until 9:00 o'clock that evening, so we could take David home with us. The whole atmosphere changed and the oppression was so heavy it was almost tangible. I thought I was going to smother.

An "English" lady, who was invited to the wedding, had a cell phone. I asked her if I could use it; I needed help fast! I tried to call Michael's so they could pray for me, but they didn't answer. I got up and walked through the house to go outside and people were in little groups talking about me.

When I passed one of the groups, they looked scared like they were seeing a ghost. I went out to the side of the house and kept trying to call. It started to rain and my cap got wet and blotched, and I wasn't fit to be seen. Then a big group of boys and young men came around the corner. They were my relatives, my nephews and nieces' husbands, etc.

As they passed me, they mocked me and called me names. I didn't know where to go so I went around to the screen door to give the phone back.

I asked my sisters, "What shall I do?" They just shrugged their shoulders, because they would get in trouble if they were seen talking to me. So, I went out to a shed, hoping the mockers wouldn't find me. To my surprise, my nephew, Levi Kauffman, was standing there alone and he said, "Mattie, Mattie, come here," and he started talking as fast as he could.

First, I want to say that the Holy Spirit had been working in my sister Malinda's family, and had already done a work in Levi's heart. They left the Amish community three months after we did. Levi had been very popular and a leader in bad things. He basically did what the boys wanted him to do.

Now he told me that all day long he had refused to participate in anything they wanted him to do, and then he refused to go along to their beer party. He said that a little earlier before I had walked in, a group of boys came up to him and wanted to know why he was behaving this way. He said something to the effect that he's decided to follow Jesus.

They acted really scared and said, "Do you have Aaron Mattie's belief?" It is customary to call the wife by the husband's name first. Then they scattered as fast as they could. Now they were afraid of him, but he was just fine with them when he was doing all the bad things.

CHAPTER TWENTY TWO

Rumors and Conversions

I want to relate some of the more serious things that were said about me. This comes directly from someone who was standing with the two older men when it was said. He is now an ex-Amish and that's how I found out. They had heard the rumor, and it was just a rumor, that I had told someone I was filled with the Holy Spirit. They were laughing and joking about it and making fun of me when one of them said, "I wonder how that would feel?" and they kept on laughing some more about it. That sounds to me like blasphemy, but God is the judge of that.

Also, in a preacher's meeting where they were discussing me and the Bible I carried, the bishop said, it's alright to have Jesus, but that I didn't have to be so *treiflen* (in German), or silly about it.. Sorry folks, I will be silly about my Jesus any day. I know my God is more pleased about that, than being "silly" about the rules. The funny thing is that during those one and a half years of rumors, I wasn't talking to anyone except my family. The first thing that really caught my children's attention was when I told them what Michael had said about some very frightening things that were happening in the world.

I said that I'm not afraid at all and I can't wait for more bad things to happen so we could get closer to the time of Christ's return. Wow! Looking forward to when Jesus will be coming? What a mind boggling thought! I didn't have a lot to do with their conversions, except that I prayed for them a lot. It was one miraculous event after another. Lorene was first and she said very little to Aden, just prayed.

The Holy Spirit changed him one night when he was lying on the ground gazing at the stars, in awe. As he saw God's great big universe he realized how small he was and how great our God is.

Then God placed deep within Aden's soul this truth, that Jesus would have died for him, if he had been the only person on earth. That was a dramatic life changing event. Miriam was next. I had mostly told her the same things I told Lorene about four months prior and the Holy Spirit did the rest.

She worried that William would never see the truth, so she also just prayed. One night, several months later, she prayed desperately before she fell asleep. Much later that night, she woke up and William wasn't in bed. He had lit an oil lamp in the living room and was reading the Bible! That's where his conversion began. Now, I've written about Norman's, Marilyn's and David's conversions.

Betty had a new birth experience about a year before and didn't tell anyone, but with not much spiritual food and the correct teaching she almost died spiritually. Imagine her joy when everyone else found salvation, too.

Esther, Alfred's wife, also had a new birth experience in 2001, when she went through some terrible things. The community accused her of having an affair with the driver who was an older man, old enough to be her dad. They even spread rumors that little Rosie was his child. Esther suffered so much that it caused her to turn to the Bible.

She was also overjoyed when the rest found the truth. Alfred had known the truth, too, but didn't actually receive the new birth experience until a year later.

Another joyous event happened a year after we left, when my sister, Dora, her husband, Lester Kauffman, and family of 12 children left the Amish community. They lived in Charlotte, at the time and we had no contact during that year.

I think you can see that the Holy Spirit had his way without a lot of help from me. Ivan and Alma are still Amish and the shunning has caused unspeakable pain for him, and for us, as well. Imagine what he has suffered when losing his family and hearing all those terrible rumors about them! I'm looking forward to all my loved ones being together again one day where no religion or tradition can separate us.

This is one of those things that is difficult to write about. Right after we left, the rumors took on a new twist, and these were the most painful ones.

People were saying that some of us were seen naked out on the trampoline because when we read the Bible we wanted to do like Adam and Eve in the garden. It was like making fun of our Bible reading. Also, they said when we got together to worship we would all dance together in the nude. This was so humiliating!

One form of communication was a circle letter. A circle letter involves about 7 to 10 friends or it could be family members who live far apart. When it gets to your house you write a page and add it to the letter, then send it on to the next person. When the letter comes around again, you take out your old sheet and replace it with a new one you have written and send it on again. This type of communication is helpful if you don't have a phone.

An ex-Amish friend told me later that she had read a circle letter and someone wrote about all this juicy gossip. Then, another woman wrote and asked if they really believed all that. A woman from our community wrote, "Oh, yes." She believed every bit of it and she even added some more. I had never before known that so many rumors could develop out of absolutely nothing. Then, as they spread from community to community they accumulated more and got much bigger than where they started.

This is another thing that was said about a year before we left. It was going around that I drank some sort of brown liquid, like a witch's brew, that had caused me to get this strange belief.

This rumor is probably still being strongly believed today. After we were at that revival, they claimed that the driver who took us had been waiting outside the tent in his van. The story went that when he came back from the revival, he told the other Amish what a frightening thing he had witnessed while sitting out there. Supposedly, he saw a bunch of little black demons running all around the tent.

So, now they had proof positive that we had been in the devil's camp! I wanted to tell them that apparently, the demons couldn't get inside.

Michael and Bethany were our drivers and they enjoyed that revival as well as we did.

This is one thing I heard being preached in the Amish church. A preacher would get up and say what we came to church for; like to do the will of God, or something similar.

Then he'd say that the devil came right along with us this morning, and he's right here. I would imagine I saw demons riding on every buggy driving in the lane that morning. I wish they could know the victory we can have in Jesus. That would be a big step in the right direction.

They also preached that on judgment day you were going to be put on a scale. Then, if the scale didn't balance because of some weakness you had in your life, Jesus would put his foot on the scales until it balanced. So, if you had done all you could you would enter heaven. That would strengthen their "hope," since they believe they can't know that they're going to heaven. I wish they could understand that Jesus paid it all and that salvation is a free gift, if we would only receive it.

I want to clarify another thing concerning the rumors that developed about four years after we left. They always expect that things will go badly for us, and that our eyes will open and we will desperately want to come back, but we can't.

So this is how one rumor went. Someone saw me sitting beside the road and they stopped and saw that I had a bunch of empty boxes all around me.

Supposedly, I told them to light the boxes; that I wanted to be burned up, because I knew I was going to hell anyway. They just love this type of rumors to strengthen each other against ever doing what I did. I just want to assure the ones that believe those rumors, that there isn't one bit of truth in them. I've never, for one moment, regretted what I did, even though it hurt tremendously and I surely miss my friends and relatives very much.

I will not trade that for the freedom I now have in Christ Jesus. Now I don't have to run and hide the open Bibles when I see a buggy coming down the lane.

I am praying that you, too, will be released from that bondage of fear. I hope you will search the Scriptures and find the shining Light that will guide you on your journey to freedom.

ABOUT THE AUTHOR

I was born to an Amish bishop and his second wife. At age 51, I did the unthinkable and left the Amish community. Most of my family left at the same time. We were all banned and are still being strictly shunned. Without my Jesus, I would not have had the strength to do it.

This is the first book I have written. God is so good. He gave me the courage and the wisdom to tell my story.